BECOME THE BRAND OF CHOICE

Make Your Name a Powerful Brand

...and Earn Millions!

BY JASON HARTMAN

Third Edition
Revised

Published by
The Hartman Media Company

Cover design by Professional Imaging Consultants
Printing and page design by Printmedia Communications

Edited by
Richard H. Meyerson

What others say about Jason Hartman
and his trend-setting new book:

Become the Brand of Choice

Make Your Name a Powerful Brand
...and Earn Millions!

"Giving to others is the tenet which drives humanity to spiritual growth. Commerce and business have been slow to learn that giving to others is the surest way to financial success. I am happy to see a book like yours taking the lead."

LESTER BROWN
Internationally Acclaimed Motivational Speaker and Author

"Your segment was the highlight of the program. People were inspired and touched by your excellent presentation."

SHEIDA HODGE, PRESIDENT
Professional Training Associates Co.

"Jason can build consumer trust into a strategic tool for business growth better than anyone I've ever met!"

SCOTT LAING
iSucceed.com

"Thank you for a very well planned and motivating program at the *Breakfast of Champions*. Your style is very natural and believable."

NANCY THOMPSON, VICE PRESIDENT
World Savings Bank

"As evidenced by outstanding feedback on your presentation, we benefited tremendously from your presentation. Thank you for the knowledge and expertise you share with fellow Realtors."

MIKE REAGAN, VICE PRESIDENT
RE/MAX Conventions, Inc.

"Thank you for participating in our programs. Your program was enlightening and very entertaining as well. We look forward to working with you on future projects."

DENNIS HARROUN, DIRECTOR
Real Estate Television Network

"Indeed, you are one of the finest practicing Realtors® in the business."

CHARLES STRICKLIN, PRESIDENT
Stricklin & Company

ACKNOWLEDGMENTS

There are many people working behind the scenes who often make those in the spotlight look better than they truly are – to those who have helped me with this project, I say thank you for your effort and dedication. I don't have enough space here to acknowledge the many individuals who have been my inspiration through the years. My sincere gratitude goes to all who have assisted me in this work and in my life's journey.

To my editor, Richard Meyerson, who has shown the patience of a saint throughout my many additions, deletions and revisions; to my family and friends for their support, especially but not exclusively to Jeff Meyers, Cary Bren, Frank Verrill, Ed and Angie Wright and Rudy Svrcek; and to my co-workers and staff who keep the wheels turning. Special recognition goes to Hillary Nichols and Robin Anderson for their invaluable suggestions as the final draft of this book was being forged.

I also want to thank the authors, speakers, and mentors who continue to have a profoundly positive effect on the course of my life, including, but by no means limited to: Zig Ziglar, Denis Waitley, the late Earl Nightingale and Og Mandino, Jim Rohn, Anthony Robbins, Les Brown, Stephen Covey, Dennis Prager, Tom Bay, Harvey Mackay, Terri Sjodin, Howard Brinton, Hal Morris, and Wayne Dyer.

Thanks to all, you are a true blessing, you helped make it all possible and I am truly grateful for your unwavering support.

TABLE OF CONTENTS

*"Never doubt that a small group of thoughtful,
committed citizens can change the world.
Indeed, it's the only thing that ever has."*

Margaret Mead

∽ Introduction ∽
Becoming the Star You Are

WELCOME! You are about to join me in a modern-day crusade to bring a human face back to the forefront in the rapidly changing world of sales and marketing. Over the past several decades, I believe many marketing executives have drifted into a state of detachment that has created a widening gap between companies and their customers. The loss of credibility has led to suspicion and conflict in the marketplace where once there existed trust and good will. However, I believe that with sensitivity and the use of new technologies, we can help close the gap, and hopefully reduce the level of mistrust that exists in many segments of the marketplace. If you apply the techniques I present in this book, you will have a profoundly more satisfying career and your personal life will be even more fulfilling than it is now.

My two-pronged formula for successful marketing is based on the building of "mass" personal relationships, and the creation of what I call "personal brands" (a personal brand is all the things that represent you and that people identify with you). In other words, people will do business with you because they recognize you, and trust you. The processes you will use to build your personal brand are the sum and substance of this book. Please do not be disappointed when you discover that many of the principles discussed in these pages are not new. Many can be found in some of the oldest writings known to man, such as early religious manuscripts and those of the great philosophers and thinkers of the past. All have one overriding characteristic in common. They are designed to show us how to attract wealth, happiness and fulfillment into our lives by helping others achieve those things for themselves. On the other hand, many techniques that I discuss have been derived from cutting-edge 21st century communications technologies, which have become widely available only within the last few years. By carefully applying these concepts, you can grow your business and increase your income and, perhaps most importantly, enrich your life with quality relationships and personal balance.

> Personal Branding can grow your business and increase your income and, perhaps most importantly, enrich your life with quality relationships and personal balance.

For a variety of reasons, the loyalty and trust that attract people to their favorite brands, or favorite stores, have been diminished in the hectic pace of modern business dealings. Marketing strategies are now less frequently based on building loyalty, trust, or friendship between buyer and seller than had been commonplace in the past. The emphasis has shifted to mass marketing, low prices, large selection, and shopping convenience. While I have no doubt whatsoever that all of these things are important and valued by customers, I believe that the human touch is what ultimately makes the real difference, and that consumers appreciate being known by name, rather than by number. They prefer being greeted by a live voice, a warm smile, and a human "experience." While this may be practical for small local businesses, however, the challenge is to give large corporations and retailers the same capability. That is what I will address in this volume.

Personal Branding as a stand-alone concept is just now coming into its own. Traditionally, "tooting one's own horn" was frowned upon as a sign of conceit and an over-active ego. Now, however, it is considered good business to build a personal brand to show consumers how your virtues can help them, and to enable you to compete successfully in an ever-more-crowded and competitive marketplace.

As you read this book, you might be surprised by its simplicity, but don't let that distract you. Many of us have been conditioned to think that if something isn't complex, it must not be worth considering, but that's not true at all. Yes, this book is rather simple - it's just common sense in many cases.

In today's rapid-fire world, I have observed that personal relationships in business are taking more and more of a back seat to impersonal spreadsheets and statistical marketing studies. It's as if we don't have the time anymore to be "nice" to each other. Fewer transactions are consummated by a handshake. Multi-page contracts, warning labels, disclaimers, and disclosure statements dominate our ever more litigious society. Distrust, suspicion, disloyalty, dishonesty, litigation, misunderstanding and disservice are often the unfortunate consequences. Could it be that trust and loyalty, honesty and integrity take too much time and effort to build and nurture? Does the breakneck pace of modern business cause these virtues to be brushed aside for the expedience of making a sale? It's often said that, "You have to take time to smell the roses." Well, I believe you first have to take time to plant the roses!

I have decided that the best way to write this book is with one foot in the 21st century, and one foot in an earlier, friendlier time. There are already so many books on trendy hot-concept marketing techniques on the bookstore shelves, and so many get-rich-quick schemes have been promoted, that we tend to lose sight of the basics - the tried-and-true methods that have stood the test of time, and that actually work!

ONE OF THE REVOLUTIONARY EFFECTS OF COMPUTERS IS THAT THEY HAVE LEVELED THE PLAYING FIELD.

I don't mean to imply that Personal Branding and relationship marketing will bring you instant success (they won't), but their beauty is that they can be used successfully by virtually everyone. Combined with modern mass-communication techniques that I will soon discuss, the individual or small business practitioner is now able to effectively stay in touch with hundreds, even thousands, of people at a time, just as larger firms have been able to do. This gives you an important advantage in building your Personal Brand, or in competing successfully with much larger and wealthier firms.

The fundamental principles and high-tech methods used in modern relationship marketing and Personal Branding can eliminate endless hours of cold-calling and uncomfortable high-pressure closing. Automation, if used properly, gives you "scalability" which can vastly increase your ability to reap financial success in your career without becoming a workaholic, or subordinating your personal life to the demands of your career or business.

I want to emphasize early in this discussion that as valuable as the new systems are for your business, they must be used judiciously since they vastly increase your capability to contact your customers and prospects, and there is often a fine line between being helpful and being a pest. As much as I like voice broadcasting as a marketing tool, for example, I recognize that people have an inherent dislike of mechanical systems that tend to dehumanize both the sender and the recipient of the message. No one likes to be bothered by telemarketing messages, and that is especially true of recorded ones. Yet, as consumers, we want and need information, and we desire value, selection, and a variety of products and

4

services in our everyday lives. Since we can't avoid being consumers, I think it is safe to say that we would prefer that our buying decisions be made in an atmosphere of friendly relationships coupled with valuable information, rather than detached anonymity.

A good example of this is illustrated by the remarkable success of multilevel, or network marketing, which evolved from the notion that most of us prefer personal contact with someone we know and trust to being an "account number" in some distant company's computer. Billion-dollar network marketing companies such as Amway and Herbalife operate on the rather simple notion that consumers, if given a choice, would prefer to buy and sell within a "relationship" network. My conception of relationship marketing and Personal Branding go beyond most multilevel marketing systems, however, since many people are turned off by the pressures inherent in network marketing. For those who choose to sell within a networking organization, rah-rah rallies and the outlandishly high incomes of the company's top producers can be energizing, but they can also be discouraging to the vast majority of people who are not able to consistently perform at such high levels of production. You must be careful not to let unrealistic expectations discourage you from applying the successful strategies that these companies employ.

Most people dream of wealth and success, but very few are able to get beyond the dreaming stage. That's because it's so much easier to dream than to do. The reality of achieving success where none existed before comes by eliminating or changing unsuccessful habits and behavior patterns, and replacing them with new, more effective ways, which must then be consistently and persistently applied. For many of you, fundamental shifts in the ways you normally do things or the context from which you operate may be necessary. If you have ever tried to change an ingrained habit, or a personality trait, you realize how difficult it can be. It's therefore not realistic to expect that by merely reading a book such as this you will be able to create change in your life. It will take a diligent effort to alter the basic ways that you live. Reading alone will not do the trick. Since any significant change in your life requires commitment and constant reinforcement, this isn't the type of book that you should read through quickly and put aside. You won't receive its full value unless you internalize the ideas and make them your own. Refer back to this volume often. Keep it on your desk, rather than on your bookshelf. Write in the margins, and highlight sentences that are meaningful to you. My hope is that in writing this book, I will be able to give you a means of achieving your financial goals while building quality relationships.

YES, I SAID WRITE IN THE MARGINS!

I am living proof that it is possible to change. It is by committing to conscientiously apply new ideas that I was able to move beyond my one-bedroom apartment and become a self-made millionaire. No, I did not have an auspicious start in life - I wasn't born with a silver spoon in my mouth. I arrived in Orange County, California without money, and I knew no one. I started my real estate career in the ultra-competitive, high pressure Southern California market, but I was undaunted because I believed I could succeed anywhere, and that the road to wealth is paved by effective self-promotion and close personal relationships. Applying my people-oriented concepts, my belief in the power of relationships as a marketing tool was firmly established.

In building my business, I was struck by the fact that so many people preferred to buy from someone they knew, rather than from a large faceless corporation. After all, people relate to people much better than they relate to brands, logos, companies, buildings or slogans. I also noticed that the better known that someone was, the more people seemed to want to do business with him or her. The top producers (the "stars") in business had became local celebrities, and seemed to draw business to themselves as if by magic. I learned important lessons about the value of personal notoriety, and I incorporated those ideas into my Personal Branding methodology.

Human beings are social creatures, and many billion-dollar companies have been built on that aspect of human nature - that people need people. With that in mind, the selling process can become a win-win situation for both the seller and the buyer when conducted within the framework of mutually advantageous relationships.

In writing this book, I did not want to re-invent the wheel, so I modified and adopted a number of concepts used successfully by corporations for many years. Many other methods that I discuss are less familiar, because the technology that enables them did not exist until just a few years ago. Finally, some of the ideas you will discover in these pages are personal outgrowths of my own relationship marketing / Personal Branding methodology that has enabled me to build my multi-million dollar real estate organization.

While people tend to relate better to other people than to product brands, it has long been known that consumers tend to develop powerful loyalties to certain products. For example, a smoker will smoke one brand of cigarette for the remainder of his or her (ever shorter) life. Automobile owners will often buy another from the same manufacturer without even considering alternative marques. Before the advent of the modern superstore, people had their favorite neighborhood hardware stores, where they were addressed by their first names, and where they could go not only for hardware and tools, but also for advice on their do-it-yourself projects. People shopped at the same friendly corner grocery stores for years, never considering switching to the new supermarket in town.

In the days before mega-stores became dominant, consumers were often as loyal to their brands and their stores as they are to their friends. In fact, many of the neighborhood storekeepers

TO WHICH
BRANDS ARE YOU
LOYAL? HOW
COME?
actually did become their friends. I think we have lost something in today's homogenized world. I admit that because I'm a relatively young guy, I can't honestly speak from personal experience. However, from what I've read and heard, it seems that there was more honesty, and relationships of all types were more solid, a few decades or more ago. A handshake really meant something, and a person's word was his or her bond. Friendships and business relationships were more "local," and they seemed more solid. Friends did business with friends, and loyalties ran deep. These shopkeepers may not have realized it, but they had built powerful personal brands at the same time they were developing personal relationships with their customers. Do I think that the answer to business success, then, is a return to the values and methods of the "olden days"? The answer is "yes...and no."

Yes, in the sense that personal relationships are powerful, and essential to build a business and ensure its longevity, and should be an integral part of doing business. No, in that the old style of doing business is not scalable and can't easily be extended to hundreds, or thousands, of customers over a wide geographic and demographic spectrum. There just aren't enough hours in the day to deal with everyone one-on-one. That's where Personal Branding enters the mix. A brand synthesizes a relationship on a mass scale.

> As we will soon see, a Personal Brand takes
> the place of an actual personal relationship
> by making it seem that there is a relationship,
> when in fact, there is none!

Life was simpler, and there were fewer choices to make, in "the good old days." Service was all-important, and the customer had to be satisfied. But consumer buying decisions were just as much conscious choices among competing alternatives then, as they are

8

now. When consumers were faced with a difficult choice, they often chose to do business with people they knew and trusted. Buying decisions that involved several friends offering the same products or services were often very difficult decisions to make, indeed!

In the days of relationship based selling, one often heard the words "trust," "friendship," "loyalty," "warranty," and "guarantee." These words aren't spoken as frequently anymore, and aren't used extensively in modern American retailing. Warranties are still offered of course, though often with much fine print and many exclusions. Many merchants stand behind the products they sell. However, the significance of manufacturers' warranties has been blunted in the eyes of the consumer since it has become clear that one of the main functions of the warranty registration mail-in card (which is the most visible manifestation of the warranty in the eyes of the consumer) isn't so much to stand by the product, as to gain information about consumers for marketing databases. Consumers are suspicious of these data-gathering functions since the information is then often used to target them for additional sales pitches, or worse, their personal information is sold without their permission to other companies for those companies' own independent marketing efforts.

To make matters worse, many firms now focus the training of their sales personnel on selling and closing techniques, rather than on product knowledge and information. With more and more emphasis on quantity of sales, rather than quality of service, the gap between the customer and the seller has widened until an "us vs. them" mentality has developed. The "win-win" relationships of the past are rapidly losing out to casual cash-and-carry transactions. Many of my recent business transactions have all had to be done at least twice because of vendor foul-ups before they were able to do it "right." Not only is that a tremendous waste of resources, but it is also indicative of today's "it's good enough" attitude in business. My personal feeling is, good enough is never good enough!

Unfortunately, many consumers choose to forego service in return for low prices. The resulting price war has caused some retailers, pressured by razor-thin margins, to pull most of their salespeople off the sales floor, to cut costs. Customers of these stores are no longer fitted for clothing, unless they do it themselves. Operation of complex electronic consumer products is not explained or demonstrated - it's left to the buyer to try to decipher increasingly incomprehensible operating instruction manuals. Instead of providing qualified salespeople in the store, these companies are spending millions of dollars to determine market trends and buying habits. They may have forgotten that their customers are individuals, not mere demographics or psychographics.

Companies are able to offer low prices because of the economies of large-scale production and low labor costs in certain foreign countries, which allows consumers to simply dispose of their widgets when and if they break, and buy new ones. All-inclusive warranties and long service relationships are quickly becoming a thing of the past. Consumers have come to accept poor service, or worse yet, no service at all, as the tradeoff for low prices. Not too long ago, I was kept on hold for nearly an hour by my Internet service provider when I called to speak to a customer service rep. Disposable products may be a good thing, but unfortunately, one of the casualties is customer relationships. Relationships should never be treated as "disposable."

The small "mom-and-pop" business that was traditionally built on relationships with its customers has been the most visible casualty of this trend. The advent of the superstore brought a wide variety of goods and prices with which the small shopkeeper could not compete. Don't get me wrong - I'm not totally opposed to chains and superstores. They have introduced valuable marketing concepts such as price-point advertising, broad selection, large market research studies, price leaders, telemarketing, sampling, direct mail circulars, and preprinted newspaper and periodicals inserts. While personal service is often an unfortunate casualty in the expensive hunt for more and more customers, superstore companies have devised useful ways to find and retain new business in an increasingly ultra-competitive environment. So I'm not suggesting that we discard all modern merchandising methodology and technology and go back to "the good old days." I simply believe ways can be found to improve the business environment without compromising the feeling of personal service, relationships, and a sense of community. The larger scope of today's business world does require that ways be found to allow the traditional ideas to be leveraged, to work on a much larger scale ("scalability").

Consumers are becoming increasingly resistant to high-pressure and impersonal sales tactics. Many people no longer answer their phones at dinnertime, thinking that it is probably a telemarketer on the other end of the line. Most people don't even bother to open the "junk mail" that fills their mailboxes every day. If asked about the billboard around the corner, many of us couldn't make an intelligent guess as to its message. Annoying commercials on radio and television no longer register their pitch. They actually turn us off instead, encouraging "channel surfing" or the use of instant-replay digital recorders such as Tivo's to skip the commercials. Rather than selling us their products, these methods of marketing are becoming so ubiquitous and abrasive that they simply have less impact in the midst of all the commercial noise. It's ironic that companies are spending fortunes on advertising campaigns that may alienate many of their customers.

There is little doubt that these marketing methods, although highly successful when first conceived and applied, have lost much of their luster. They are increasingly perceived as annoying and invasive. They are also very expensive. Due to decreasing effectiveness, some companies are cutting back, reducing their telemarketing departments, or abandoning their expensive full-color junk mail in favor of new advertising technologies (check www.adage.com).

I believe that the tide is turning. Customers want a sense of personal service again in the clothing store. They want knowledgeable and non-invasive automobile sales people, not "closers," or "high-pressure sign-today" types. They want the professionals they deal with, such as their doctors, accountants, Realtors® and stockbrokers, to know their names, and to know their needs, wants and desires. Many clients would like the people who take their money to also take a personal interest in them as human beings.

This isn't rocket science. It's really as simple as it sounds. I call the process Golden Rule Marketing. Just put yourself in the shoes of your customer, and ask,

"How would I like to be treated if I came into my store as a customer?"

It isn't difficult to address customers politely, or to show an interest in them. A word of caution is in order here, however. Don't be pushy, don't pry, and don't ask questions that are too personal (relationships take time to develop; you have to earn your customers' trust before you enter their personal space). Don't crowd them, physically or verbally, or make them feel uneasy, or they will hightail it out of your place of business and never return! Practice treating your customers and prospects the same way that you would like to be treated, and you'll soon get the hang of it.

As wise as it is to apply Golden Rule Marketing, I suggest you take it one step further and put your customer's needs and desires before your own - I call this *Platinum Rule Marketing*. It's not so much treating your customers as *you* would like to be treated - it's treating them as *they* would like to be treated. Find out what is important to them, and before you open your doors for business, design your product or service to satisfy their needs. I look at the automobile industry as a prime example. For many years, American automobile manufacturers operated on the premise that they could design and build the kind and style of vehicles they wanted to build, and customers would just buy whatever they found in the showrooms. Then, European and Japanese companies came along and asked, "What kind of vehicles would you like to buy?" They designed their products to meet the wants and needs of their customers, and grabbed a huge chunk of the domestic automobile market away from the out-of-touch American companies before they knew what hit them. Once lost, customers are very hard, if not impossible, to regain.

Many businesses, especially those selling services or big-ticket items such as automobiles, have become so obsessed with market share and have focused so intently on garnering a huge customer base that it is practically impossible for them to have meaningful relationships with individual customers. Small companies can have a real competitive advantage over their large competitors if their goal is to build personal relationships with their customers. That may ultimately be the best way for a small business to compete successfully with the large corporations. Developing relationships with customers, and an effective personal brand, can be the salvation of the "little guy," the start-up, or the sole practitioner.

However, using such a traditional one-on-one approach does not work well after a certain "critical mass" of customers is reached. Sheer numbers can doom a company's efforts to successfully put a relationship-marketing program in place. In many such cases, companies may resort to lowering prices in an attempt to build customer loyalty. The primary drawback of basing loyalty on low prices alone is that when your competitors drop their prices below yours, many of your customers will abandon you. If a price war

For many years, American automobile manufacturers operated
on the premise that they could design and build the kind and
style of vehicles they wanted to build, and customers would just
buy whatever they found in the showrooms.

develops, no one will win because every merchant's profit margins will shrink toward zero. Here is where Personal Branding becomes indispensable, as the brand substitutes for the one-on-one relationship. Just as people buy from people they trust, they will buy brands they trust. If you personally are a brand, people will buy from you. I will discuss this subject in greater depth later on.

In his book *Tender Warrior: God's Intention For A Man*, author Stu Weber does an excellent job of outlining what I have adopted as my core philosophy. In essence, he says (and I paraphrase):

Weber, Stu. Tender Warrior: God's Intention For A Man, Questar Publishers, 1993.

We often misplace our priorities. We focus myopically on acquiring houses, cars, stock portfolios and bank accounts and piling up a whole lot of stuff. We imagine we will find happiness through these things, when in fact there is no lasting happiness, or status or security, if we don't have satisfying relationships. We think, 'If I have a good income, if I've put away money for the kids' college educations, if I have an adequate life insurance policy, I'll be a success and I'll be happy'. We focus on the wrong things in our quest for happiness and fulfillment. I think if we spend more time nurturing relationships, we will be wealthier in material things as a natural consequence. Character traits such as kindness, integrity, fairness, and honesty are the kinds of things that outlive a person and leave not only a physical monument, but a legacy as well.

It is that basic philosophy that I have sought to incorporate in this book. My hope is that you will not only agree with my methods, but that you will apply them in your life and in your career. As I've already said, that will require some effort on your part, because you may have to change some aspects of the way you live your life. For example, to achieve positive outcomes, you need a positive attitude, which must go beyond the smiley face that you wear for just a few hours of the day at work. You really need to be and feel positive. If you tend toward pessimism, I suggest you have some work to do to make the most effective use of what I will be sharing with you in this book. This book is not intended to be a get-rich quick scheme. This is a book designed to add riches to your life by having you take inventory of yourself, and make the necessary personal adjustments so that you can use relationship building to expand your business and your personal life.

It's hard to pass along advice on how I think you should behave without sounding "preachy," and I don't want to do that, but there comes a time in many people's lives when they must just bite the bullet and change what isn't working. In the final analysis, trying to avoid or take shortcuts around life's potholes really doesn't work. For example, consider the diet pill industry - a multi-billion-dollar business built on the fact that people want an easy way to avoid the work and discipline of exercise and healthful eating. Or, in our financial endeavors, how many of us have chased foolish "get-rich-quick" schemes because we haven't saved, invested and spent responsibly, or because we want "something for nothing," or because we are so impatient and immature that we go into debt because we want something NOW, without working and saving until we can afford it?

The "positive attitude" and other "feel good" books that fill bookstore shelves certainly contain many important messages and helpful advice, but I believe that if we smile just long enough to take our customers' cash, and then take no further interest in them after they walk away, we have deluded ourselves into thinking that we are on the road to success. These superficial relationships will soon evaporate, just as a lasting spousal relationship isn't built only on the loving behavior we exhibit during courtship. Long-term relationships in business, just as in courtship, are built on the mutual respect, interest and caring that we demonstrate over months and years of interaction. We have short-circuited the process if our only interest is to sell the customer, since our real goal should be to resell the customer over and over again. That is what customer loyalty is built on. That is what successful

HONESTLY CARING ABOUT YOUR CLIENTS IS KEY.

relationship marketing is all about. That is what personal branding is all about. That is what this whole book is all about. Without building a caring bond of friendship and honest communication, there will be no customer loyalty, and with your competitor's next big low-price promotion, your customer will disappear.

The sequence of learning from this book is nearly as important as the concepts themselves.

1   We must examine our own inner nature first, eliminating any "shortcut" and "get-rich-quick" mentality. We should prepare to put others first in our lives through honest caring and frequent communication.

2   We need to return to the traditional loyalty marketing concepts that worked so well in the past. We need to know how to keep our customers loyal to us even when bombarded with tempting sales, savings and selection from competitors.

3   We need to understand and use the best of the mass marketing techniques developed during the past two or three decades. Many of these methods are very effective in attracting and retaining new customers.

4   We must stay up-to-date with new technologies, and how they can be applied to building our customer base, satisfying our customers, and communicating with them. Remember that "education is the shortest distance between where we are and where we want to be."

5   We should also never forget how important it is to have more time for ourselves, to lead balanced lives, maintain our health, seek lasting happiness and nurture satisfying personal relationships.

Have fun and enjoy the journey!

Part One

Get Ready...

Get Set...

-Go Get 'Em!

*"Committing yourself is a way of finding out
who you are. A man finds his identity by identifying."*
— Robert Terwilliger

❧ Chapter One ❧
Making Success Your Lifestyle

SOMEDAY I'LL ...

*There is an island fantasy
A "Someday I'll," we'll never see
When recession stops, inflation ceases
Our mortgage is paid, our pay increases
That Someday I'll where problems end
Where every piece of mail is from a friend
Where the children are sweet and already grown
Where all the other nations can go it alone
Where we all retire at forty-one
Playing backgammon in the island sun
Most unhappy people look to tomorrow
To erase this day's hardship and sorrow
They put happiness on "lay away"
And struggle through a blue today*

But happiness cannot be sought
It can't be earned, it can't be bought
Life's most important revelation
Is that the journey means more than the destination
Happiness is where you are right now
Pushing a pencil or pushing a plow
Going to school or standing in line
Watching and waiting, or tasting the wine
If you live in the past you become senile
If you live in the future you're on Someday I'll
The fear of results is procrastination
The joy of today is a celebration
You can save, you can slave, trudging mile after mile
But you'll never set foot on your Someday I'll
When you've paid all your dues and put in your time
Out of nowhere comes another Mt. Everest to climb
From this day forward make it your vow
Take Someday I'll and make it your Now!

DENIS WAITLEY
(Courtesy of Denis Waitley, the Waitley Institute)

I believe that success isn't just a tally of net worth; it's a state of mind. It's a journey, not a destination. It's active - a verb, not a noun. It's a very personal thing. It's not something easily quantified. We short change ourselves if we try to measure the level of success we have been able to achieve in our lives by comparing ourselves to others, though it's human nature to define who we are and what we are by observing those around us, and determining where we fit on the informal scale of success which we each create in our mind's eye. However, we must never lose sight of the fact that what's right for someone else may not be right for us. We must live our own lives, seek our own goals, and develop our own relationships. And when our brief journey on this planet is over, we should be concerned about our legacies - how will we be remembered after we are gone - as selfish, self-centered users and abusers, or as individuals who made contributions to a better world, whose lives really meant something more than how terrific we were as consumers and acquirers of things.

Sam Walton, the founder of the Wal-Mart retailing empire, enjoyed driving a beat-up old pickup truck that he'd owned for years. When a reporter asked the billionaire why he continued to drive the old truck when he could afford any vehicle in the world, Sam replied simply, "It fits," leaving the reporter to ponder the response. I don't think the reporter thought that answer made a whole lot of sense, or a good story, but I disagree - I think it was rather profound. If Sam liked his truck, whose business was it to disagree with him? He liked it, it made him happy, and he was not out to fit anyone else's idea of what he should be driving. It fit him, and that's all there was to it! He didn't feel a need to prove his success by comparing himself to others, or trying to fit into other people's expectations.

WAL-MART IS ONE OF THE LARGEST CORPORATIONS IN AMERICA.

I am writing this book about relationship marketing and Personal Branding, which are about fitting well with your customers. It is about assisting them, caring about them and communicating with them. When your customers also feel this way about you, and they need a product or service you have to offer, they will come to you and only you. And you won't have to chase after them to get their business!

Doing business this way is very satisfying, and it is not difficult if you go about it correctly. On the other hand, it is very difficult if you do it wrong. Think of how easy it would be for your personal relationships to go "on the rocks" if you forget a birthday and habitually come home too late. Before you know it, your relationship is in trouble. If you don't quickly repair the little things, the relationship can be permanently damaged, or slip into a state of apathy and disregard. If left too long without rejuvenation, the relationship ends and the parties go their separate ways, seeking someone else to satisfy their neglected wants and needs.

It is very much the same way in business. "Business" does not take place in a vacuum - it is people relating and dealing with each other. Do you think people leave their humanness at the door when they are involved in business dealings? Of course not! What is important to them in their everyday lives is just as important when they engage in commerce. It is a matter of fundamental human nature. Tend to your clients' and customers' needs, communicate with them often in a caring and friendly way, and those important business relationships will be nurtured, and will flourish. The opposite is also true: forget a kind word, an encouraging e-mail or telephone call, or an occasional lunch, and the relationship will fade, slipping further and further from you, until it is gone forever.

Suppose you have a very important task ahead of you. Imagine you will be competing in the Olympics, or entering the boxing ring to fight for the heavyweight championship of the world, or you will be singing a lead role in "La Boheme," or you will be making a sales presentation to an important client. Would you do any of these things without training, rehearsing, and practicing? Of course not! In a similar vein, to be successful at Personal Branding and relationship marketing, you need to condition yourself. You need to develop the habits that will enable you to stay in touch with current and former clients, while continuing to develop new relationships and new clients. The beauty of doing business in the 21st century is that whatever your business, product or service, you can now effectively remain in contact with hundreds, even thousands of people at any given time. In a later chapter, I will go into more detail on the incredible power modern technology gives you in your efforts to stay in touch with large numbers of customers and prospects.

How do you get to Carnegie Hall? Practice, practice, practice!

24

We'll also discuss ways to become more aware of the desires and needs of others, and I will show you how to use this information to build a powerful platform from which to develop successful business and personal relationships.

In this book, I am going to show you how to influence others to buy from you, deal with you, and consider you a friend. You will come to believe, if you don't already, that you are valuable, that what you have to say is valuable, and that your product and service are valuable. You will also come to believe that you are doing your customers a favor by sharing yourself and your products with them!

GETTING YOURSELF COMMITTED

My background is in real estate. As a believer in the existence of the bell-shaped curve, I didn't want to become a member of the vast, mediocre "flock"; I wanted to be the best, the most successful Realtor® that I could possibly be. Having read Napoleon Hill's classic book, *Think and Grow Rich*, I realized that there are common traits shared by successful people, and I wanted to identify those that applied to real estate brokerage, and apply them in my own career. So when I first started in the business, I researched local real estate firms to identify the top producers, and find out what they were doing to achieve and sustain their success (it was as a result of this exercise that my fascination with Personal Branding developed).

As I got to know the top sales producers in my firm and in other firms, I noticed something that most of them had in common - they were deeply committed to their personal success, to their clients, and to their community. They were genuinely committed, from the innermost core of their beings. After reading scores of personal improvement books, and listening to hundreds of audiotapes, I knew that total commitment would be necessary to achieve my goal. As I am sure you have heard it said, "If it is to be, it is up to me." I knew that if I weren't committed to my own success, nothing would happen, because I couldn't expect anyone else to do it for me. I also realized that I couldn't achieve success in a vacuum - that I needed the support and cooperation of others - my co-workers, family, and friends (I did not want to become a rich, miserly hermit). As for commitment, I also needed to be totally committed to the satisfaction of my clients and prospects. Yes, I knew I needed to be rich in friendships and good relationships - not only with my co-workers, family, and friends - but also with my clients.

While I was totally committed to do the work necessary to be successful in my career, I realized that without complete satisfaction on the part of my clients throughout the entire process, my commitment to my career didn't matter much. I always keep in mind that I am nothing without my clients and that my clients are people, and they react and interact just like the people in my personal life (in that regard, I'll bet far fewer spousal relationships would end in divorce if both parties were truly committed to each other's happiness).

That being said, what if you aren't committed to client satisfaction? How do you become "committed" if you do not actually feel that way? Not easily - it's sort of like falling in love with someone you don't really like. But it can be accomplished. Commitment arises from motivation - if you don't passionately want something, you will probably not have the degree of commitment needed to overcome the inevitable setbacks you'll encounter, and you may not have the determination to stick to your goal.

Since commitment derives from your belief system, which empowers and supports you, and your beliefs can be changed, you do have some degree of control over how you perceive and react to your world. Beliefs, attitudes and conditioning are the primary determinants of behavior, so if you are able to modify your beliefs and attitudes, you should be able to alter your behavior. An increased level of commitment can then become a natural outgrowth of a new set of goals based on your new priorities. As a first step in this reorientation process, it is important to be introspective and honest with yourself. Look at yourself in your mind's eye mirror and thoroughly examine your present attitudes and beliefs. This self-examination process is essential, because for commitment to work for you, it is not enough to want to be committed, or think you are committed. You must actually be committed.

But commitment isn't all that you will need to successfully implement a relationship-building program. You will also have to develop an outward-directed set of values so that you can enable your customer to "win," and feel good about the transaction he or she just engaged in with you.

Here are some helpful conditioning tips to build stronger commitments to your present clients, your future clients, or any relationship that you might wish to strengthen:

Start small and build

Small things make a big difference in relationships, especially if they aren't a "once-in-a-lifetime" occurrence. Always be on the lookout for small ways to strengthen client relationships. Use the phone, a postcard, an e-mail message, or a thoughtful little gift (this has become so easy using Amazon.com's gift click service). There are several websites that make it easy to send e-mailed greeting cards or automatic gift deliveries (check www.egreetings.com). Make it a goal to constantly build those important personal and business relationships. Your success depends on it!

Conditioning Tips
for Strengthening Commitments

- Start small and **BUILD**

- Use existing commitments

- Community involvement

- Strengthen belief system

- Practice good habits

- Continue prospecting

- Set goals to score

- Results-oriented

Start with existing commitments

Follow through with the relationships to which you are already committed. Concentrate on strengthening those that mean the most to you. Experiment with, pay close attention to, and learn from your actions and the other party's reactions. Don't procrastinate - not being prompt at returning phone calls, letters, and other commitments tells people: "You really aren't very important to me."

Start with community involvement

Get involved in your community. Since your clients and prospects are all part of the community at large, if you work to improve your community you can improve your individual relationships as well. By the way, I mean be actively involved in the community, don't just talk about it - volunteer for civic projects, be active in your religious organization, host charity events, etc.

Giving, with no expectation for personal gain, is the golden rule of strong relationships. Contributing your time is one of the most generous ways you can give. Look for quality opportunities, and contribute your time and energy to a volunteer project, even a small project, as often as you can. The interesting thing about giving is that more often than not you eventually receive something in return, though what you receive may not be a direct result of what you have contributed. This is partly due to the fact that a basic aspect of human nature causes people to want to respond positively to acts of generosity by others.

Strengthen your belief system

Your belief system is constantly being challenged by an imperfect world. For example, you may feel that people as a whole are fundamentally good, but each bad guy headlined on the 11 o'clock news chips away at that belief. One way to reinforce such beliefs is to embrace your religion, or spirituality, on a regular basis, so that your faith in the goodness of man (or whatever your belief happens to be) is reinforced in spite of adversity. Find as many ways as possible to strengthen your beliefs so that these challenges do not overwhelm you, and cause irreparable damage to your soul.

Develop, and practice, good habits

Strong relationships don't just happen because you want them to; they develop because of your commitment to nurturing them. If you are in sales, and you had a good month, what is your tendency? Take time off to go to the beach, golfing, or the mountains? It's okay to reward yourself for a job well done, and that is fine for a little while, but then it's time to get back to work. Don't get into the habit of slacking off. Prospecting and marketing are the lifeblood of selling, and if you don't prospect and promote continually, you will have roller-coaster income, and you won't succeed in the long run. Your level of success is directly related to the amount and quality of your prospecting. With today's technology, for the first time, you can make prospecting virtually automatic. We'll discuss this in a later chapter. Remember that *if you continue to prospect and market your Personal Brand when times are good, times will never be bad.* Repeat that statement a few times a day.

There is a classic poem about the importance of commitment that we should tape to our refrigerator doors and cubicle walls. I'm not sure who wrote these lines, so I ask the author's pardon for not giving the appropriate credit:

DON'T QUIT

When things go wrong, as they sometimes will,
When the road you're trudging seems all uphill,
When the funds are low and the debts are high,
And you want to smile, but have to sigh,
When care is pressing you down a bit,
Rest, if you must - but don't you quit.

Life is queer with its twists and turns,
As everyone of us sometimes learns,
And many a failure turns about
When he might have won had he stuck it out;
Don't give up, though the pace seems slow -
You might succeed with another blow.

Often the goal is nearer than
It seems to a faint and faltering man,
Often the struggler has given up
When he might have captured the victor's cup.
And he learned too late, when the night slipped down,
How close he was to the golden crown.

Success is failure turned inside out -
The silver tint of the clouds of doubt -
And you never can tell how close you are,
It may be near and it seems afar;
So stick to the fight when you're hardest hit -
It's when things seem worst that you mustn't quit.

- Author Unknown

AIM FOR THE GOAL...AND SCORE!

The next step in establishing an effective relationship marketing and Personal Branding program is goal setting. I'm familiar with several goal-setting systems, and I'd like to share with you one that has worked well for me. Here are the guidelines for effective goal setting that will help you develop clear, concise goals.

Be results-oriented

Your goal statement must focus primarily on the desired result, and it must specifically state in the present tense what it is you want to achieve, as if you have already achieved it. A concise one-sentence statement is usually adequate. For example, rather than saying, "My goal is to make $200,000 this year," the statement is more effective when you state it this way: "I'm on track to earning $200,000 this year, and I'm enjoying the benefits of my high income every day." Remember that your sub-conscious mind is very gullible. It can't tell fact from fiction. So you can fool it into thinking you are already at your goal, and it will direct your behavior accordingly. You can thereby create your own reality by telling yourself you've already achieved it. This process works for both short-term and long-term goals.

Use a specific time frame

Define the specific time frame for the achievement of your goals. When you have a time reference, it adds a dimension of urgency to the goal-setting process. It also gives you a logical framework for dividing, planning and pacing the steps necessary to achieve your goals. For example, rather than saying, "My goal is to lose ten pounds," the statement is stronger when you rephrase it this way: "I have already lost ten pounds, at the rate of two pounds per week.

For every pound I lose, I feel stronger and have more energy." You have established a realistic time frame for the realization of the results of your goal statement, and by avoiding time ambiguity, you lessen the chances of procrastination or abandonment of the goal.

The goal should be measurable

You must define a clear way to measure your progress toward the achievement of your goals, and specific targets at which to aim. When your goals and your progress are measurable, you are more easily motivated to work toward them, because you can monitor your results and take corrective action if you are off course. Also, by having immediate feedback of your progress, you reinforce your commitment to your goals. Instead of saying "My goal is to start a savings plan this year," the statement is stronger when you rephrase it this way: "I've saved one hundred dollars from each paycheck for a year, and I'm enjoying the security of knowing I have a growing savings account."

As you set your goals, write a detailed statement of the sensory impressions you will feel when you actually realize each goal. Be as specific as possible: What will it look, feel, taste, sound and smell like? Also, detail the emotions you will experience upon the realization of your goal. Next, write a statement of the "payoff," or the positive consequences you will derive from achieving the goal.

Test the sensory aspects of your goal statements with questions such as these:

- Is this something I really want?
- Is this possible (realistic)?
- Will it change me and help me grow?

ELEVEN STEP PROGRAM

Set Example

Stay Positive

Take Action!

Assign Life Goals

Create Plan

Visualize Your Ideal Self

List Resource Assets

Review Goals

Write about 5 Goals

Set Specific Time Frame

Make To Do List

If your goals are to take root in your subconscious mind, and activate your nervous system to set you on a path to take action toward their achievement, they must be imbued with rich sensory detail. Remember that your subconscious mind cannot tell the difference between reality and vivid imagination, so the more vivid and realistic you make your mental images, the more likely you are to fool your subconscious into believing your goals are already your reality. If your subconscious believes you have already achieved your goals, it will direct your conscious mind to behave accordingly, and your behavior will hasten the actual realization of your aspirations. Just as the little acorn is the seed of a giant oak tree, our goals are the seeds of our reality.

It has been said that a person without goals is like a ship without a rudder. It's not a good idea to go through life rudderless. To help you navigate life successfully, I will now give you an eleven-step method for goal achievement. From my own experience, I've found it to be a very effective system.

THE ELEVEN-STEP PROGRAM

Step One...

Make a detailed list of all the things you want to do, be, and have. Create in your mind the people, places and feelings you want to experience. Use your imagination to do, or be, or have anything and everything. Do not limit yourself! Remember to include things in all areas of your life, such as: career, relationships, finances, leisure, education, spirituality, retirement, and family.

Step Two...

Put time limits on each goal - one month, six months, one year, etc. If you find that most of your time limits are long-term, break your goals down into smaller sub-goals. Generally speaking, you will be more likely to achieve large goals if they are tackled in easily accomplished smaller segments. Remember that "the best way to eat an elephant is one bite at a time." On the other hand, if you find that too many of your goals are short-term, decide which is the most important, and prioritize them. Then focus on those at the top of the list, doing one thing at a time. If you get too scattered, or have too many unfinished projects, you will lose your focus and become ineffective, frustrated, confused and discouraged. Harry Emerson Fosdick once said: "No horse ever accomplishes anything until it is harnessed; no steam or gas can drive an engine until it is confined; no Niagara is ever turned into light and power until it is channeled; and no life ever grows great until it is focused."

Step Three...

Select five of your most important goals. Write a few concise paragraphs about each of them. Describe how each will look, feel (physically and emotionally), sound, taste, etc. Involve all of your senses as completely as possible. Create a vivid mental image of each goal as it is achieved. The longer and more detailed your descriptions are, the better. Use powerful and compelling adjectives to describe the changes that have taken place in your life because you accomplished these goals (use plenty of imagination). Read these descriptions to yourself several times a day, every day, emphasizing what the achievement of each goal will mean to you, and why you must have it. You will be much more motivated and effective if you have a compelling reason for making the effort, rather than just doing it.

REMEMBER, YOUR SUBCONSCIOUS MIND CANNOT TELL THE DIFFERENCE BETWEEN REALITY AND VIVID IMAGINATION!

Step Four...

Review your goals against this checklist:
- Are they specific?
- Are they positive?
- Are they consistent with your values (not your friends' values, or the medias', or your parents', but your values)?
- Are they clear to the senses (sight, sound or feelings)?
- How will you know when the goal is achieved (is it measurable?)?

Step Five...

List the tools, abilities and resources you have, or to which you have access. You have many resources at your disposal, and you may not even be aware of all of them. Be honest with yourself when you list your talents and abilities. List all the resources available to you for each separate goal (your resources include all the people in your life who could help you in some way). You may have a slightly different list for each of your goals.

Step Six...

Describe the type of person you need to be to accomplish your goals. Find successful role models, and read about and study their lives and their teachings. Remember that in life, as in the laws of physics, for every action, there is a reaction. If one of your role models has accomplished something that you would like to accomplish, just do what he or she did, and you should get the same, or a very similar, result (similarly, if you continue to do something that doesn't work for you, you will continue to get unsatisfactory results).

Keep in mind, however, that there are always elements of special talent, luck and circumstance, which you may not be able to duplicate or control. For example, suppose you have always dreamed of being an opera star. You have researched Maria Callas' life story and begin to copy her behavior. You try to do everything that Callas did on her road to stardom. Except for one little detail - you can't sing. No matter how hard you try, or how long you practice, or how many important people you know, you still can't sing. In this case, you'd better not quit your day job. You will never be another Callas. Or, suppose you want to be a great philanthropist like Andrew Carnegie. But you're broke. You can do everything Carnegie did, but unless you somehow become very wealthy, you will not become a great philanthropist. Or suppose you have always had a burning desire to be Queen of England. You can emulate Queen Elizabeth to your heart's content, but without the circumstance of royal birth, you have no chance of becoming Queen of England. Of course, these are extreme, even ridiculous, examples, but I want to point out the importance of being realistic and honest with yourself, or you will set yourself up for frustration and disappointment.

In general, before we can have something, we must do something, and before we do something, we must be something. Zig Ziglar said, "It's not what we get by reaching our goal that counts, it's what we become just by trying."

Step Seven...

Create a detailed step-by-step goal-achievement plan. List what you need to do today, tomorrow, next week, or next month. Break every goal down into daily activities and do something every day to advance yourself toward that goal. Remember, read your sensory goal statements every day and visualize yourself as already having achieved your goal(s). You must come to believe them, and that each and every goal you've set for yourself has already happened, or is happening right now.

Step Eight...

Be willing to take prudent risks (taking risks does not mean being reckless). Step outside of your comfort zone. When in a new endeavor that involves uncertainty, start small and build on your successes, always going forward in your actions. You can't continue doing what you have always done, or nothing is going to change. It's foolish to expect different outcomes if you persist in doing the same old things. In baseball, you can't steal second base while keeping your foot firmly planted on first base. Expecting success in achieving your goals without doing something different and being willing to take some risks is like sitting in front of an empty fireplace and expecting to get warm.

Step Nine...

Take action! There is no substitute for action. Nike (the shoe company) hit the nail on the head with their sales slogan, "Just Do It!" If one of your goals is to lose weight, you will need to get your butt off the couch, push yourself away from the dining table, get on a diet, and start a fitness program. You can start slowly, but the key is to get started. Then, follow through and make your program an integral part of your lifestyle so you do not lose your momentum or commitment to your goal.

You must take some action on every goal every day, even if that action is just to read your sensory goal statement, so you have some positive reinforcement of your commitment. If your goal is to save money, start when you get your next paycheck. Drive to the bank, open a savings account and make a deposit equal to your goal amount. Follow up with a deposit every time you get paid. Consider yourself one of your most important creditors, and you must pay yourself just like you must pay your mortgage or rent, your phone bill, or your electricity bill. Convince yourself that if you miss a payment, you will take yourself to court to collect the debt you owe yourself.

Step Ten...

Stay prospective. Try to anticipate positive developments, and facilitate them. Once your goals are verbalized, written, visualized, and you believe they will happen, just let them happen, and enjoy your progress and the daily changes that are occurring in your life. Harold Melchert said, "Live your life each day as you would climb a mountain. An occasional glance toward the summit keeps the goal in mind, but many beautiful scenes are to be observed from each new vantage point. Climb slowly and steadily, enjoying each passing moment. The view from the top will be a fitting climax for the journey."

Step Eleven...

Set an example. Let others see the progress you are making, not by boasting or merely saying you're going to do something, but by living out loud, so to speak, so that your personal or professional life-changes are evident to your friends, family and associates. People will start to change the way they perceive you - they will start to see you as the person you intend to become rather than as you were. The ways that others interact with you will change as you change, and this will reinforce the new directions that you are taking.

It's interesting how pursuing your personal goals starts to affect others in your life. A few paragraphs back, I said that if you don't take control of your future, others will determine it for you. Now, by taking charge of your life and the direction it takes, you are changing the lives of others who work and live with you as they adapt to your new reality. Don't you find that process fascinating?

"The secret of success in life is for man to be
ready for his opportunity when it comes."
- Lord Chesterfield

~ Chapter Two ~

Quit Talking and Do It!

Getting Out of Your Comfort Zone

The next step I suggest for building a successful life is moving outside of your box, stepping outside your comfort zone. Most of us believe that there are limits on what we can do, and on how much we can achieve in our lives. Fortunately, most of these limits are self-imposed, or have been programmed into us by our parents, teachers, clergy, spouses, bosses, etc. I have good news for you. You can eliminate most of those limitations. Have you ever watched the Olympics? Haven't you been amazed by the stories of super-athletes who have overcome seemingly overwhelming physical or mental adversity to become the best in the world at what they do? Do you think they would have reached such high levels of achievement if they had accepted the limitations (real or imagined) that others told them would keep them from realizing their dreams?

I view life as if it were like an onion, consisting of a series of concentric layers. Imagine that you live within one of those layers. Some of us live within the innermost, most confining layers, and others live within the outer, larger layers. The layers form the boundaries, real or imaginary, that circumscribe our lives. Each layer contains a limited amount of material wealth, quantity and quality of relationships, and opportunities. The larger, outermost layers will contain greater potential wealth, opportunity, and relationships. Those individuals who live within the small, inner layers can only achieve the limited amount of wealth and success that is available in that layer. Those who live within the outer, larger layers have much greater opportunity. To a large extent, we choose our layer or context, or have had it chosen for us by our parents, teachers, clergy, etc. If we desire more in our lives, we will have to either maximize that which is available within our particular layer, or move beyond, into a larger layer and an expanded context. How do you think a person becomes a larger-than-life figure in sports, politics, business or the arts? They lived in, or moved into, a larger layer! You can do it, too! It isn't easy, but in order to achieve real growth in our lives, it is vital to step out of our comfortable inner layers and take the risks associated with stepping over the boundaries into the larger, outer layers (the layers are, in reality, very porous - you can move in and out at will).

One of the things that keeps people from moving into the outer layers is fear of the unknown. They wonder what it will be like living outside their familiar surroundings and comfort zones. They're afraid they may not be able to survive there. Like many people, I have always had a fear of heights (being afraid of heights is just one example of the complex psychological phenomenon that can include various fears such as fear of failure, fear of rejection, fear of risk, fear of getting hurt. Fears are not just simple little phobias; they can permeate our lives in ways we are often barely aware of). As I started coming to grips with my fear of heights, I realized that it was not just going to go away by itself, and I wanted to rid myself of it. I worked hard to overcome this fear as much as I could by not avoiding high places, but actually seeking them out whenever possible.

THE FEAR OF PAIN IS USUALLY GREATER THAN THE PAIN ITSELF!

44

I don't usually do things gradually, because I'm impatient for results. So I decided I'd really take the plunge, literally, by jumping out of an airplane (oh, by the way - I would be wearing a parachute). In any case, this was really stepping out of my comfort zone: thirteen thousand feet in the air, and then jumping out of an airplane and free falling toward earth! My resolve began to disappear soon after takeoff. I thought about changing my mind about how badly I wanted to achieve my goal - maybe it wasn't really that important to conquer a fear of heights! But then I remembered that I had told several friends what I planned to do, and I needed to "save face" (I highly recommend that you make public declarations of your goals as a way to put pressure on yourself to achieve them).

With a deep breath, I stepped out of the plane and fell like a lead weight at more than 100 feet per second. I couldn't turn back now! I was committed, whether I liked it or not. After what seemed like an eternity, the parachute opened. I was momentarily living in a larger circle than I had ever been in before, and as I floated toward earth, I was surprised that I was already starting to feel at ease in my new, expanded context. I had taken a giant step forward, and was

beginning to feel the exhilaration and freedom of having overcome another restrictive barrier. Since that day, places that previously seemed very high did not seem so high any longer. Have I totally overcome my fear of heights? Not completely, but I did learn another important lesson about fear - the anticipation is usually far worse than the reality. I had stepped outside of my comfortable little box and briefly experienced the world outside. The jump boosted my confidence on the ground as well, just as I had hoped it would. I realized that larger "onion layers" were basically no more threatening than the one I was accustomed to. As long as I was "brave" enough to venture out, life could become so much more fulfilling!

While comfort zones may give us a sense of security, they can clearly become huge obstacles in the way of our achieving our goals. We can eventually become so deeply entrenched in the ruts we have dug that we simply can't climb out. Years of suffering the disappointments and frustrations of broken dreams, and "living lives of quiet desperation," as Thoreau said, can sap our will and enthusiasm for life, and we just settle for whatever we have. We may then feel that we have no choice as to whether or not to step outside our boxes, or we lack the motivation to do so.

A friend of mine wrote the following little story, and I want to share it with you.

THE BOY IN THE BOX

Once upon a time, there was a boy who lived in a box. It was really quite a nice little box, having food, and all sorts of playthings and comfortable furniture inside. It had one little window through which the boy could watch the world outside. There were no doors, but the boy didn't mind, because within the box was everything he needed, and he was content to watch the world through the window.

One sunny day, a beautiful princess rode by on a glorious white horse, and she stopped to examine the strange little box by the side of the road. She was startled when she peered in the window and saw the boy inside. He was just as surprised to see her.

"Who are you?" he asked. "What do you want?"

"I want you to come out here," she said. "It's a shame to be inside that box on such a beautiful day."

"I've never been out there," he answered. "There are no doors in my box."

"What a pity," she whispered, "the world is such an exciting place, filled with beauty, adventure and love."

The color left his cheeks. "Please don't speak to me of those things, because then I become aware of my walls. I have lived in here quite comfortably for a long time and I no longer notice the walls. They have kept me safe."

"Safe, perhaps, but have you ever soared on the wings of love, or tasted the fruit of passion, or experienced the exhilaration of discovery?" she asked.

His eyes darkened. "Please don't ask me those things. They arouse desires within me, and make me long for a door."

She pressed her face closer to the window. Her crystal blue eyes danced with the promise of things the boy had only dared to dream of. He reached out and gently touched her cheek, and from that moment on, he was never again happy in his box, and he searched endlessly for a door.

- RICHARD MEYERSON

It is easy to ignore the self-imposed walls that we have built around ourselves, which so often limit us to lives of boredom, mediocrity and complacency. We might even convince ourselves that we prefer the "safety" of the status quo. Why, after all, should we take risks and rock the boat when we have enough to sustain our basic lifestyles?

As a child, we were told stories like "Little Red Riding Hood," which hammered home the message that we had better "stay on the path," or terrible things might happen to us. Staying on the path may keep you safe, but the realities of today's rapidly changing business world require that we step off the safe path and take risks in order to meet the challenges of intense competition. If we stay where we are out of fear of change, we will fall further and further behind. For example, consider the number of retailers that have failed because they persisted in doing what they had always done rather than adopt innovative merchandising methods, or find ways to satisfy changing consumer tastes. Huge companies such as K-Mart and Montgomery Ward didn't adapt to the changing lifestyles of their customers, ultimately losing all or most of their market share, ultimately filing for bankruptcy and often going out of business entirely.

The cruel joke is that comfort zones are largely illusory. In the world of business today, nothing is a "sure thing" - just ask the laid-off employees of the thousands of companies that "downsized" their staffs, or went out of business, during the past few years. Many of these people were career employees with twenty or more years of service to their companies. Unemployment is some reward for years of loyalty to their employers!

I recently heard of someone who had left a lucrative sales position to take a routine and rather tedious job. When asked why he had made that unusual career change, his answer was rather straightforward. "I hated cold calling," he said. He's not alone. Like the safely encapsulated boy in the box, he had sought the comfort of dealing only with his regular, established clients and avoiding the uncertainty of stepping out of his box to prospect for new ones.

However, unlike the fellow who chose to take a lower paying position rather than cold call, I believe that type of fear is largely a matter of perception, and can be overcome with just a little effort. Look at a cold call as just an opportunity to meet someone new. If done in a proper and non-threatening manner, your cold call could well result in meeting someone who welcomes you and your business. Of course, many of these calls will result in rejection, and you will encounter many rude people, but that's true of life in general, isn't it? It's not realistic to expect a new friend, or client, to develop out of every chance encounter - but some do, and isn't it worth putting up with the losers to find those few new friends, and good customers, who make the entire process worthwhile?

I believe that action eliminates doubt. If you are uncomfortable with cold calling, but decide to do it anyway, try practicing first with people you already know, using pre-scripted opening lines and conversation starters. You can start to call strangers after you are more comfortable with the cold-calling process (I also believe that strangers are friends you haven't met yet). If you offer a personal benefit on the first call, rather than trying to "sell" something, you will be amazed at how quickly you can step out of your comfort zone and into effective prospecting. Relationship marketing works because it offers your prospective clients something valuable. This could be anything from a free, or discount, offer to a simple compliment, but it will only work if the offer is sincere. In a matter of moments, your "cold call" becomes a "warm call," perhaps even a "sold call." Don't become discouraged. It's normal for cold calling to create high stress, fatigue and burnout. That's one reason I am so enthusiastic about personal branding and relationship marketing, which attract customers to you rather than your having to constantly "sell" to them. You will have much more control over your time, more enthusiasm, more trust, and less stress in your life.

The basic philosophy of this great nation is that there are a few things that are fundamental to our existence as human beings, including life, liberty, and the pursuit of happiness (the *pursuit* of happiness is a fundamental right, not the *achievement* of happiness). That so few of us have genuine liberty and happiness in our lives is a sad commentary on the way we have chosen to live our lives. It's so easy to fall into apathetic daily routines, and the achievement of real happiness becomes more and more remote. Apathy is the enemy of success in our careers and businesses.

KRIEGEL, ROBERT. IF IT AIN'T BROKE....BREAK IT!, WARNER

Robert Kriegel discussed this in his book, "If It Ain't Broke....Break It!" The author says, "We're in an era of unprecedented change, and it's happening so fast. The only safe course now is 'break-it thinking', a willingness to challenge the status quo. Rest on your laurels, as the U.S. automakers have done, and, like them, you'll likely (find your business slipping away to more aggressive and customer-sensitive competitors). You cannot keep doing what you've been doing. It works today, but it won't tomorrow. You've got to keep breaking the molds and fixing them."

This process is called "creative destruction," and it is what ensures progress in the economic system we have in America today. Darwinian-style evolution takes place wherein innovation and change are constantly chipping away at the status quo. If you or your business is entrenched as part of the status quo, rather than as part of the innovation and change, your fate is sealed. It is just a matter of time before you and your business are obsolete, or left behind in the dust of your more aggressive competitors.

The most effective way for the cautious risk-taker to approach new and unfamiliar situations, either in personal or business relations, is by taking small steps. For example, you may find it more comfortable to sit with friends at a seminar, but you will miss the opportunity to meet new people, gain new insights and develop valuable new client relationships. Take a small step and make an effort to forgo the comfort and camaraderie of your friends, and go sit next to strangers (and talk to them). Keep in mind that strangers are just friends that you haven't met yet!

Taking small steps also allows you to test the limits of your comfort zone, and how far it is "comfortable" for you to step outside of them. It may be perfectly comfortable for one person to speak in front of an audience of 5,000, while another might not be comfortable speaking face-to-face to even one stranger. Each of us has different comfort levels. Fortunately, not everyone needs to jump out of an airplane to overcome a fear, but each of us can, and should, be testing the boundaries of our comfort zones as often as possible.

The use of "safety nets" is another good idea when stepping out of your comfort zone. For instance, if you are planning to open a new business, it may be wiser for you to hang your sign on the door three months later, rather than right away, using the extra time to do research, market analysis, polling, evaluation of the competition, etc. This interim period of learning and research often helps you avoid expensive mistakes on the road to success. Too many budding entrepreneurs fall so much in love with their own ideas that it never occurs to them that perhaps no one else wants or needs what they have to offer.

If you're just learning to swim, it's prudent to jump from the edge of the pool into the shallow end first. Accept the challenge to step out of your comfort zone in gradual stages and small steps. Break a frightening project into small steps and usually the fear disappears. Ask yourself what you believe to be true and what you expect to happen, if you step outside of your comfort zone. That can reveal your boundaries. There really is nothing fundamentally wrong with having comfort zones, for they do serve us in a positive way by keeping us out of the trouble that can arise if we venture into areas beyond the scope of our abilities (i.e., jumping into the deep end of the pool before we learn to swim). Just as comfort zones define and settle our world, their borders can indicate what is beyond our reach, or where a comfort zone becomes a danger zone. The important thing is not to consider them safe little cocoons that may offer security and protection when in reality they may hold us back from successfully pursuing the goals we can and want to achieve.

Unfortunately, we don't always know how to evaluate what is truly "beyond our reach." Most of us can achieve so much more than we do because we are held back by a lack of motivation or low self-confidence. After being injured in a fire, doctors told pre-medical student Roger Banister that he might never walk again. But through incredible determination and faith in his ability, he forced his way into ever expanding comfort zones until he was not only able to walk, but he became an accomplished runner. In 1954, overcoming greater odds than most of us could even imagine, Banister became the first runner in the world to break a barrier no one thought could ever be broken - the four-minute mile. He ran the mile in 3:59!

In another example of unwavering commitment to one's goals, |NEVER GIVE UP! Walt Disney went bankrupt twice before he finally convinced a producer that animated cartoons could be successful. His own father had all but given up on him, but Disney believed in his vision, and persisted in the face of discouragement and apparent failure. Clearly, he was out of his comfort zone. Isn't it fortunate that Disney did not give up on his dream? The world would never have known Mickey Mouse and Donald Duck, or the theme parks, motion pictures, books, and merchandise that followed.

One common trait of successful people is that they are always seeking ways to test the limits of their comfort zones. This is what distinguishes leaders from followers, and what gives winners their "competitive edge." A critical difference between successful entrepreneurs and those who fail is that the winners hang in there long enough to reach the finish line. So many people quit too soon. They have the vision, but perhaps because of their self-imposed limits, they cannot see how close they are to succeeding. One person perseveres, testing and re-testing, while another convinces himself or herself that it can't be done - why even bother trying - no one can break the four-minute mile.

So what holds us back? One reason we stop short of our goals is the fear of failure. Suppose you do fail: you may not achieve your goal. But if you don't even try, you are certain not to achieve your goal. So what do you have to lose by giving it a shot? It reminds me of a joke: a man goes to church and prays, "Please, God, let me win the lottery." The next week, he goes back and prays again. Week after week, the same thing. Finally, one day during his prayer, he hears a booming voice, "All right, already! But first you have to buy a ticket!"

Aside from often being the prelude to success, failure can be a great teacher. Consider the example of Thomas Edison. He failed

53

in hundreds (perhaps thousands) of attempts to build a functional light bulb. Each failure was not a cause for despair, however, but for celebration: Edison knew that if that particular filament didn't work, the field of possibilities had been reduced, increasing the chance that the next try would produce a winner. Similarly, prizefighters know that they don't lose a fight by being knocked down. They lose by not getting back up. How many salespeople get past the "no's" when cold calling or prospecting? The first few "no's" discourage one salesperson and send him home packing, while they encourage another salesperson to try again, because she believes she will get one "yes" for every nine "no's." Every "no" is one step closer to a "yes." What do you really have to lose by making a second call and then a third? You don't have the client anyway, so there is nothing to lose by trying it a second time. When you are "rejected," be reassured that it's not personal. Rejection has nothing to do with you personally... it's only about your sales activities. And always remember the basic rule of relationship marketing: offer a tangible benefit and often your cold call will develop into a relationship.

The late Dave Thomas, the founder of the Wendy's fast-food restaurant chain, took a huge risk while he was manager of a successful family restaurant in his hometown. He was doing well financially, but when the opportunity to manage four failing Kentucky Fried Chicken franchises opened up, Thomas stepped out of his comfort zone and took the leap. The franchises were doing so poorly when Thomas took the helm that even Col. Harlan Sanders told him to save his money and allow the stores to close. A few years later, after much trial and error and creative marketing, Thomas had parlayed his small investment in the four restaurants into well over a million dollars. He used his new wealth to start the Wendy's restaurant chain. When he was asked why he took the risk, Thomas replied, "What did I have to lose? I was managing a small restaurant, cooking, doing dishes and scrubbing floors. I wanted to own my own business. I had nothing to lose."

Always be extending your comfort zones. Successful people always raise their own standards and expectations. Don't let a comfort zone limit you. Keep pushing the bar upward, higher and higher.

WHAT'S YOUR DREAM? WHAT DO YOU HAVE TO LOSE IF YOU PURSUE IT? WHAT DO YOU HAVE TO GAIN?

Applying What You Know

The fourth conditioning exercise I suggest to anyone who wants to succeed in relationship marketing and Personal Branding is to get the best possible education. One of the most significant factors that can limit your progress in business is a lack of knowledge. There is no excuse for ignorance. The opportunities to extend your education are boundless. If you want to learn, you can learn, no matter what your background, age or income. Every college offers grants, scholarships and student loans. Low-cost, or even free, courses are available at community colleges. The libraries are full of invaluable books. The Internet gives you free and instant access to a limitless amount of information. In today's world of instant communication and ready access to a vast array of information, there is no reason not to continually learn new things. Whereas in the past, it may have been inconvenient to go to a library, or impractical to spend a small fortune to buy books, today's technology has delivered practically all of the accumulated knowledge of the human race right onto your desktop computer. One thing is for sure - if you wish to succeed in life, you have to know how.

Success isn't an accident. It's a learned and controlled process. An interesting recent study of lottery winners in the state of Illinois offers some valuable insight. Fifty lottery winners were asked to take part in a survey to show how much of an impact, whether negative or positive, winning the State Lottery had on their lives.

55

The winners were of all ages, of both genders, and of different economic backgrounds, but the consistency of results is striking.

Out of the fifty lottery winners:

- Eighteen reported that they had more debt than they had before winning (of course, they also had more money to pay their bills).
- Seven were bankrupt, having sold the rights to their annual winnings and squandering the lump sum proceeds.
- Thirteen said the winnings had caused divorce and irreparable family conflict.
- Twenty-six reported they had no savings.
- Eleven reported wishing they had never won the lottery.
- Four had committed suicide.
- Two had started trusts to benefit the public and remained relatively unchanged by their wealth.
- Nine had taken the winnings, invested them wisely and built successful businesses.

These are very interesting findings for people who were given instant wealth without earning it, or understanding how it could alter their lives and relationships, and having no opportunity to prepare for the windfall. Apparently, having money was not as important to these people as knowing how to use it wisely. Wealth alone does not equate to success in life. Being successful (with or without money) is a process that you can't easily shortcut.

When I was seventeen, I purchased an audiotape entitled "The Psychology of Winning" by Denis Waitley. Waitley explained how a winning attitude, well thought-out goals, and the application of knowledge and experience could create a successful life. That tape had a profound effect on me. I listened to it over and over again, at

56

every opportunity. I concluded that while my formal education may have prepared me for life, just being prepared is like standing in the doorway with your parachute on, waiting for the plane to land. It is without action, without risk, and without results.

Knowledge satisfies the basic human need for fulfillment and completeness. It need not take the form of a formal college education; there are hundreds of continuing education programs offered by community colleges and private schools in your area, and it is so easy to listen to educational or motivational audio programs in your car as you drive. Nor does it take a great deal of effort to turn the television off and open a book. The information is there; we need only make the effort and retrieve it.

One of America's most powerful motivational speakers and trainers, Les Brown, describes his childhood in the poverty and squalor of the inner city. Brown had no formal education beyond high school, but he firmly believed that the fast track to success was through education. As a by-product of his dedication to self-education, he learned about the power of attitudes and mental conditioning, and how attitudes affect everything that we do, see and hear. He also learned how to think positively and constructively, and to set goals for his life. Fortunately, Brown listened, learned, and applied his new knowledge.

When Brown decided to turn his life around, he overcame his education deficiencies and began to read voraciously. Through books, he was able to expand his comfort zone and "travel" vicariously to far away places, learn Spanish, and become versed in economics and history. He vowed to help others make their lives more productive. He became a motivational speaker, and now speaks to disadvantaged groups, such as prison inmates, welfare recipients, high school dropouts, and street gangs, to motivate, encourage and educate those whose lives would otherwise be hopeless.

57

Like Brown, you must be open-minded and continue to learn throughout your life. It has been said that the mind is like a parachute - it works best when open.

Putting the Needs of Others First

In many sales positions, it is still the hard closer who earns the most income. This person uses every closing technique, and all but forces the customer to close the sale. But while it may be successful in the short run, this kind of selling is the exact antithesis of what relationship marketing and Personal Branding are all about. I don't believe the average customer wants to be sold anything. This hard-closing salesperson clearly hasn't put the client first - he or she has put the commission and sale first. This style of selling is not especially concerned with the customer's needs, unless addressing those needs advances the sales pitch and quickly gets to the signature line on the contract.

I'm not saying that learning everything about your product, or memorizing sales scripts, isn't important. I also believe that traditional closing methods, when properly used, are appropriate in finalizing the sale. What sets relationship marketing apart is listening to your customer's wants and needs, and then making the right fit for your customer, not yourself. By serving your customers' needs, and putting their desires first, you will build deeper loyalty, greater trust, and a more enduring relationship than if you just practice the "hard sell." It will also go a long way toward establishing your Personal Brand. Regrettably, the "churn and burn" approach to selling is a product of the basic greed that permeates the sales profession. It is doubly destructive, because it leads to burnout and a very unsatisfactory career for its practitioners.

Genuinely liking people and putting their needs before your own can sometimes be a challenge. You are instinctively going to dislike certain people, just as you feel attracted to others. But remember

58

that you are not marrying them - you are only dealing with them for short intervals within a business context. Learn to control your impulses, and take a lesson from the little chameleon. Just as the chameleon changes its color to adapt to its environment, you should practice changing your sales approach to adapt to your customers' personalities. Be friendly with people you initially don't like, and you may surprise yourself and actually grow to like them. Very often, first impressions are wrong, and given the opportunity, a friendship may develop. If it doesn't, you will still be rewarded with a client who wants to buy from you. The concept of making friends just for the power to influence them certainly isn't a new one, and it takes more work than traditional selling methods. The successful outcome, however, is a relationship that might last for many years, and generate more sales than the "hit-and-run" approach.

Liking people, rather than just selling to them, requires a different mind-set. Instead of just talking about ourselves, or our products or services, we need to ask questions and listen carefully and actively to what our clients do, think and say. It's not that difficult to do. It's a learned process, an exercise that you need to practice to become proficient. Here are some guidelines.

The Art of Liking People

ASK QUESTIONS. Whether this is your first meeting with a stranger, or a conversation with an old friend, practice the art of asking relevant questions that convey the impression that you are really interested in the other person and in what he or she has to say. People are usually comfortable talking about themselves (a topic with which they are very familiar), and are willing to provide a great deal of information in just a few minutes of "directed questioning." Think of yourself as a reporter interviewing people to get facts for a story. In this, you're a questioner and listener, not

59

a talker. The interviewee doesn't need to know much about you in order for you to accomplish your objective. During this "interview," you also aren't actively trying to sell anything. You are carefully listening, and asking questions to gather information, and to put the other person at ease. The whole time, you should be learning about the interviewee. Be careful that your questions are not intimidating or intrusive. You are a reporter - remember that your interview is about the other person, not yourself. Ask their names, their places of employment, ask about their families, how long they've lived where they live, and what they think about certain issues (it's best to steer clear of controversial issues, or matters of politics or religion).

RECORD INFORMATION. Have you ever been out somewhere, and someone greets you by name, but for the life of you, you can't remember him? Embarrassing, isn't it? If you have forgotten his name, you may try to fake it, but you'll probably look and feel awkward. However, if you do remember his name, and other details about him, imagine how good he'll feel, how much he'll appreciate you, and how much more comfortable the encounter will be. It's so important to remember names! Take the time to listen carefully to a person's name when you first meet him or her, and repeat it once or twice in the course of the conversation. Then make a note of it as soon as it is reasonably practical to do so (it's a good idea to carry a small notepad or recorder of some type with you at all times). This will help you remember his or her name, and associate the name with a face. In short, you cared enough about that person to form the basis of a relationship, without regard to whether or not it would ultimately lead to a sale.

BUILD A RELATIONSHIP. Mutual cooperation has become a rare commodity in the world of "sell them something and send them a bill" marketing. Find some common ground between you and your

60

client so that you can find a meaningful way to give something of value to improve the quality of her day, her career or her life. This embodies the essence of successful relationship marketing and Personal Branding - giving to others, making them happy, and helping them become successful. Your willingness to solve their problems, for example, will help cement your relationships, and will make the job of selling your product or service so much easier. They will seek you out, and recommend you to others. Such efforts also further the building of your personal brand, so that you will become known for your generosity and consideration.

For example, suppose you meet a software designer at a business luncheon. In your conversation, you mention that you know someone who might need his services. Once your new acquaintance hears that you may be sending him a referral, your relationship has begun on a positive note. The designer might know little, if anything, about you, but that's all right for now. You've extended your hand in friendship and generosity, and you will have your opportunity, in due time, to tell him all about yourself. A note of caution is in order here - don't promise a referral if you can't deliver one. Your credibility is on the line, and your personal brand is about credibility and honesty.

BE AGREEABLE. Showing genuine agreement and understanding in your new relationship is important in leading to real friendship. It also helps build your network of people to turn to for assistance when and if you need it.

Let's consider a hypothetical situation: suppose your company is supporting a local charity drive. At a fund raising event, you meet the fund raising coordinator for the first time. You have a few wealthy friends whom you think would be receptive if you ask them to help reach the pledge goal. You advise the coordinator that you'll make a few calls. Of course, he'll be very appreciative. You make the calls, and several generous pledges come in. Two weeks later, you meet again and the coordinator thanks you for your help, and finally gets around to asking you about your business. He not only becomes a client, but he also takes some of your business cards and hands them out to his friends and associates. A new and profitable relationship begins because you recognized a need that someone had, and was able and willing to assist. It was a win-win situation for both of you, and a new personal friendship may result as an added bonus.

BE HONEST AND GENUINE. Dr. Robert Cialdini coined the term *ethical influence,* which embodies a very important concept. Being able to influence others is certainly important, but not if it is to their detriment. As I've already mentioned, as you engage in commerce, you are establishing a reputation for yourself, building your personal brand. An essential component of that reputation is genuineness and honesty in all aspects of your relationships. You should encourage others to act similarly. Honesty always pays. It is never to your advantage to demean people, or gossip about them, or denigrate your company or other employees. And if you observe this type of behavior from others around you, you would be wise to distance yourself from it, and raise the level of professional ethics by politely suggesting that the individuals involved discuss some other topic.

Being genuine also means acknowledging your limitations. While it's important to be knowledgeable about such things as your industry and the latest trends, you can't possibly know everything. If you don't know something, admit it, and ask others to help you. Most people will be more than willing to help, and appreciate that you asked. They'll have much greater respect for you if you admit you don't know something than if you try to fake your way through it.

Your Personal Constitution

When I first started my business, I decided to write a mission statement, or *personal constitution*, defining who I was, what I stood for, and who I wanted to become. I thought about it for a long time. When I had refined it sufficiently, I wrote it down, and have not changed a word of it since. I'll share it with you, to illustrate what I have in mind. I suggest that you also give careful thought to who you are and what you stand for, and write your own personal constitution, to set the standards by which you will live. Mine is on the following page.

The Spirit Within You

As a final conditioning exercise, I suggest that you make a daily practice of nurturing yourself spiritually in some meaningful way. If you attend a house of worship, treat your involvement as more than a just a social activity. Develop a spiritual link to whatever higher power you may recognize, and seek guidance and strength.

There is real power in prayer, which is an extension of the power of creative visualization, and there is power in having a belief system, even if that belief system is uniquely your own. You can develop and expand that power through your association with positive, honest and ethical people. You diminish that power when you remain in the company of takers, complainers, and negative or unethical people. Choose your friends and relationships carefully, as you often take on the characteristics of those with whom you associate. It's true that "you are known by the company you keep."

In his audiotape series, *The Power of Prayer*, Dr. Larry Dossey explores the unique and vital power that comes from connecting with your spiritual self. He discusses prayer in the context of scientific principles, and describes how the physical and mystical aspects of our existence can affect our lives. He believes that no

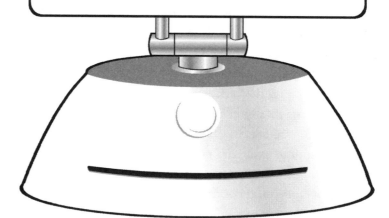

PERSONAL CONSTITUTION FOR JASON HARTMAN

I believe in living on purpose. I acknowledge that I do not really own anything material, that I am only a trustee of things until I die. The only thing I possess as valuable as my life is my integrity. I strive to live as a role model for others – with honesty, humility, and humor. I work earnestly to give back to the world at least as much as I have received. I realize that to do good, I must feel good; therefore, I will treat my body with respect and nourish myself with exercise and healthful food.

one belief system or religion has a monopoly on prayer. Anyone who has faith that prayer works can obtain positive results from it. Faith, in a business context, manifests itself as confidence in one's ability to sell, to run a company, or to be a valuable employee. It is a willingness to take calculated risks and having the patience to wait for the results.

Living by a code of ethics becomes a framework for your entire life. If you believe, as I do, that you reap what you sow, then you appreciate the way ethical behavior in all your personal and business relationships will ultimately inure to your benefit.

In developing your personal Code of Ethics, a very important distinction to keep in mind is that of the personality ethic vs. the character ethic (as discussed by Stephen R. Covey in "First Things First"). As Covey described it, the personality ethic includes all those things about the person that are essentially superficial in nature - looks, charisma, charm, having "a way with people." On the other hand, the character ethic includes such things as honesty, personal integrity, loyalty, courage, etc. As I view it, in today's ultra-competitive world, someone with a strong personality ethic will initially have doors opened for him or her, but being able to take full advantage of the opportunity and build long-term relationships with prospects will require a strong character ethic. In my business of real estate sales, for example, a strong personality ethic will get an agent numerous listing presentation opportunities, but to actually get the listings, the character traits will have to be present and successfully conveyed to the prospect.

COVEY, STEPHEN. FIRST THINGS FIRST, SIMON & SHUSTER, 1994.

For those not familiar with the workings of the real estate business, a better example may be the 1996 U.S. Presidential election. In that campaign, Bill Clinton (with his strong personal charisma) clearly and undeniably had a tremendous advantage over his opponent, Bob Dole. However, in hindsight, it is clear that Dole had the stronger character. Since voters initially tend to respond

65

to the superficial rather than substantive qualities of candidates, Bill Clinton won the election. However, as his performance in office spotlighted his character deficiencies, Clinton's charismatic appeal wasn't sufficient to ensure long-term relationships with his constituency, and he essentially squandered his popularity. By the time of the 2000 election campaign, the character issue had become so pervasive that Clinton's Vice-President, Al Gore, in his own bid for the Presidency, had become tainted by association with Clinton's lack of character and Gore was adversely affected in his own campaign. His shortage of personality ethic made it too difficult to overcome Clinton's taint and probably put the nail in the coffin for his Presidential aspirations (though his opponent, George W. Bush, was no dynamo in the personality department either, his strong character ethic was probably the determining factor in his razor-thin victory).

As a by-product of defining your personal Code of Ethics, you will likely develop a sense of appreciation and gratitude, and you will hopefully realize that a bountiful life is not your birthright. Thanking others for their support and contribution to your success is not only the right thing to do, but it will strengthen your relationships. Expressing gratitude for the opportunities in your life, the liberties you enjoy, and the growth that you hope to achieve, is equally important. Take time every day to be spiritual, and get involved in activities that further your spiritual growth, through religious or community functions, or even just by helping someone in need.

Please excuse me if I sound too "preachy." I realize you purchased this book to learn how to become more successful in your career and don't want a lecture. But I strongly believe that a self-centered, insular mentality works against a successful career. Like it or not, we live in a world of people, and we must successfully relate with them if we are to prosper. I have learned that one of the most effective ways to get out of a self-centered orientation is through a belief in something higher and more significant than yourself. You don't have to believe in a traditional God, or practice an organized religion, though they provide a whole spiritually based infrastructure and ready-made body of beliefs and traditions if you choose to embrace them.

Part Two

The Heart of the Matter

"There are no dumb customers."

- Peter Drucker

❧ Chapter Three ❧

It's All About Relationships

MANY OF THE MARKETING TECHNIQUES routinely used today weren't even available until about twenty years ago. So much has changed since the relative simplicity of the recent past that if marketing professionals who have passed to the great beyond could return, they would be amazed at the changes that have occurred in their profession! While it is certainly true that many of the basic concepts learned in business schools are as valid today as they were in the past, the practice of relationship marketing and personal branding in their modern applications has given these concepts a whole new meaning. As we will see, when employed properly, new methodologies can significantly change the way companies and individual practitioners find and retain customers.

One of the fundamental differences between modern relationship marketing and earlier traditional marketing practices grew out of the tendency for traditional marketing to view all customers as being essentially alike in their needs and wants, and as part of a large homogeneous and rather amorphous group. Our society has become so much more diverse and complex over the past few decades that a monolithic view of the market is most disingenuous. A company can no longer just fill a room with telemarketers, give them a generic script, and have them randomly call everyone in the phone book to develop leads or make sales. This simplistic approach will probably not generate results worth the costs involved in operating the program.

Of course, homogeneous market segments do indeed exist, and the wants and needs of the individuals therein do not necessarily vary significantly. Nevertheless, relationship marketing demands that companies design their sales pitches to appeal to individuals, rather than blindly using a "shotgun" approach to find customers from the general population. Toward that end, companies first need to identify their target market(s), and then build customized databases, identifying their prospects based on demographics, psychographics, and customers' individual needs and desires. To efficiently accomplish this, companies use what is referred to as a mass customization approach, because there aren't enough hours in a day to deal one-on-one with their prospects. Scalable ways must be used that establish relationships with many prospects simultaneously, in as short a time as possible.

Ultimately, a successful relationship-marketing program must result in the integration of the company's products with the values of its customers. Rather than offering its products or services to an entire diverse market, the relationship marketing approach is to identify and focus on those most likely to buy the company's products or services, and not waste time and resources on the others.

This does not mean that market "farm" areas must be limited to a particular geographical size, or to a finite number of consumers (the term "farming," for those of you who are not in sales, refers to the prospecting process, that is, your efforts to obtain new clients through such activities as e-mailing, direct mail, cold calling, or distributing flyers within a defined geographic area, or to a particular group of people). Farms are not restricted in size by any rules or precedents. They can be as small, or as large, as you wish, as long as they are manageable within the context of your resources and capabilities. What farming in a relationship marketing context does, however, is require you to tailor your product or service to your clients and prospects, and offer it to them as individuals rather than as an undifferentiated "market." In "markets," individuals vary widely by age, gender, socioeconomic status, occupation, needs, wants and desires, and just about every other factor you can think of. A non-targeted approach to marketing assumes that in every heterogeneous mass market, there are individuals who will want to use your product and service. While the premise of this concept might very well be true, it results in "shotgun" marketing approaches that are often too expensive and ineffective, especially for the sole practitioner or small-to medium-sized business. This includes such things as mass mailings, television advertising, print media advertising, billboards and Yellow Pages advertising.

It surprises me that many experienced marketing people consider a one-to-three-percent return from a direct-mail marketing campaign as a success. Just because this response rate may be the statistical norm, it doesn't mean it's a desirable strategy. What about the 97-99 percent of wasted time, effort, and money that's inherent in such campaigns? While the inherent "waste" may have become an accepted industry norm, wouldn't it be better to reduce the waste and use the savings for more productive purposes?

Another example of the inefficient use of resources can be found in outdoor advertising (billboards). Billboard sales reps sell to clients based on what they refer to as "number of impressions." This means that if 5,000 cars drive by the billboard every day, and each car averages 2 people in the car, the "number of impressions" created by your message is 10,000 per day. While these are impressive numbers (they can be much larger along heavily traveled highways), the reality is that most people don't even notice the billboards. It is naïve to assume that as people drive by a billboard, they make a conscious effort to read it. And even if they do read it, its message often does not register as a conscious memory, nor do they jot down the phone number or web address while driving along in traffic. The fact of the matter is, as in most mass media marketing efforts, you must generate a huge number of impressions, so that a very small percentage of them will actually register with customers and lead to sales. Once again, a tremendous amount of waste is inherent in the process.

While this type of marketing may be suitable for large corporations with multi-million dollar brand-building budgets, it is not suitable for the smaller firms among us.

The same can be said for the apparently vast exposure offered by network or cable television. In this case, the ad rep makes the sale on the basis of audience size, or number of viewers. As an advertiser, it is possible to target your message by buying time on specific programs, targeted to a particular audience, or at particular broadcast times, or you can purchase "run of station," or ROS spots. These spots are less expensive because the television station plugs in your message at its own discretion, based upon availability of time in its broadcast schedule. While your message may thus wind up being shot gunned to a huge audience, your return is usually quite small (anywhere from one to four percent of the audience). Once again, waste can eat up 96-99 percent of your advertising dollar, since your message will not be wanted, or be relevant, to most viewers at these arbitrary, usually non-prime-time time slots.

Relationship marketing differs markedly from these inefficient mass marketing techniques. The shotgun approach is replaced by systematic, individualized targeting. The delivery mechanism is rarely the mainstream media (although some relationship marketing techniques can be effective when executed through the mainstream media). The effectiveness and efficiency of relationship

74

Sales Per Impressions vs. Impressions

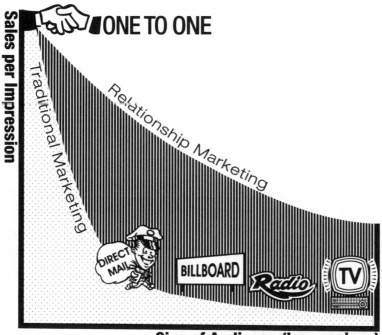

marketing is much higher than more traditional mass marketing methods since most of these techniques are permission-based, and are therefore far more relevant to your audience ("permission based" means that the viewer has affirmatively requested that your information be sent, or has voluntarily chosen to watch your ad or read your materials). Of course, this results in lower promotion costs and less wasted effort.

Another fundamental difference between relationship marketing and more traditional approaches is in the nature of information gathered, and how it is used to build long-term relationships with customers. In sales, prospecting can't be avoided, and it must be employed in a relationship marketing context just as in traditional marketing methodology. Once the prospect becomes a customer, however, the relationship marketer focuses on building a long-term relationship with benefits to both the company and the customer. An example to illustrate this point might be as follows: suppose your local telephone company, in its bid to sell you telecommunications services, also offers to broadcast your sales message to its other customers. Would this be a benefit to you? Of course it would! The relationships between you and your customers and prospects are enhanced through the phone company's offer, and your relationship with the phone company is enhanced by the additional benefit you enjoy by utilizing its services. If you adapt techniques such as this in your own business or career, and are able to benefit your customers and clients, you will never want for sales and referral business. It's a classic win-win situation!

Understandably, this mass customization approach can be a formidable undertaking, requiring that a company keep large quantities of detailed information about the needs, choices, preferences and behavior patterns of possibly thousands of customers. Of course, the entire process requires much more than that. Successful relationship marketing requires that you not only know how to gather and store the information, but how and when to use it to your advantage. Companies must maintain a comprehensive data warehouse on their customers, which is developed through a process known as data mining.

Until recently, the facilities for mining and warehousing vast amounts of information simply didn't exist, or the resulting database was too cumbersome to be used effectively. The development of modern computer technology, and especially internet-based application service providers (ASP's), has made large-scale data management possible for individuals and the small- to medium-sized firm.

TEN CENTRAL CONCEPTS

#1 - Customers and Clients

Relationship marketing and the development of a strong Personal Brand significantly alter the traditional definition of "customer." If you've been around for a while, you may remember when you could walk into your local bank or grocery store and be greeted by your first name. The owner or staff of your favorite restaurant probably knew you and remembered your favorite menu selections. Getting to know customers, and treating them as if they were special, was the way business was conducted, and is the essence of today's relationship marketing and Personal Branding. Take interest in your customers and clients, not just because they are potential sales, and money in your pocket, but also because you have a genuine interest in getting to know them, and in satisfying their needs. Tailor your product or service for them, and develop strategies for dealing with each of them on an ongoing basis.

Relationship marketing also redefines the term "customer service." Rather than simply dealing with customer complaints, as

Ten Central Concepts

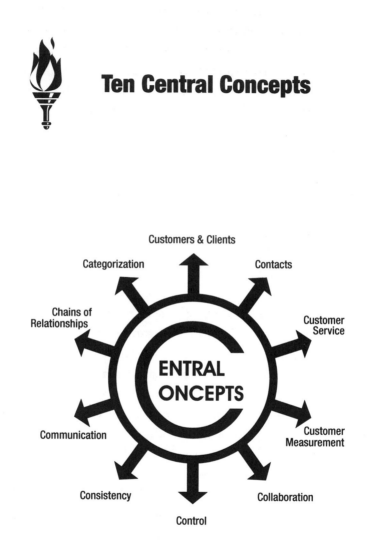

most customer service departments are designed to do, a relationship marketing approach utilizes the customer service department as more than merely a reactive function that responds to mistakes and shortcomings in how your business is conducted. It becomes a proactive function of the company as well, by taking the initiative in maximizing customers' experiences with the company and its offerings. For example, it may offer free upgrades for previously sold products, or send out notices of special sales for past customers. Not only is that type of initiative important for financial reasons, but also there are ethical and legal considerations as well, such as in voluntary recalls of defective products. Your responsibility as a businessperson is to offer a valuable and useful product or service in return for fair compensation.

#2 - Contacts

The process of developing contacts generally starts with the all-important first call of traditional marketing. Suffice it to say, the first call should not be a random or chance event. It must be planned and coordinated with forethought and purpose. I'm sure you've heard the old maxim, "You don't get a second chance to make a good first impression." Well, the initial contact call is your first and probably only chance to make that good impression, and it must be a work of art, or you could lose the prospect forever. It must quickly grab the prospect's attention, keep him or her interested in what you're saying, and eventually develop into a sale, and hopefully, a long-term relationship.

Ideally, your customer should inquire about the cost or benefits of what you are offering, even before you've mentioned them. When this request to purchase or use your product is initiated by your prospect or customer, the sale is as good as made. You might follow up "warm" or "hot" leads, generated by yourself or others. Perhaps

79

you cold-called, treating the process as a "numbers game," much as a direct-mail campaign might aim for a 1 to 3 percent return.

Personal Branding and relationship marketing work differently in that instead of trying to sell your product, or convince people to buy it, your first effort is to sell yourself. As you introduce yourself, you offer something more meaningful to your prospect than just a product or service - you offer a potential friend. The way to do this at the earliest stage of the sales process is to offer your prospect something of value, or a benefit, above and beyond the product itself. It could be expertise, experience, knowledge, or in some cases, it may simply be the interest and friendship you show your client. This can be accomplished on a one-to-one basis, or a hundred-to-one, depending on the nature of your service or product, how it is designed to meet customers' unique needs and wants, and the technology used in the sales process itself. In a recent television ad campaign, my real estate firm offered a free booklet designed to help homeowners prepare their homes for sale. Many people requested this valuable information, and a number of new client relationships were formed. Had the ad just told the audience about us, it's not likely we would have had this result.

To be successful, you must proceed slowly. The first contact should be made with no effort to sell anything. You should just seek to ascertain the client's needs and desires. However, it is quite possible that the prospect will want to buy your product or service on the first contact. Don't become so engrossed in building a relationship that you forget that the ultimate goal is to make a sale. So if the prospect wants to buy right away, don't discourage him or her. More often than not, however, prospects will not purchase from you on your first call. This is probably because they don't know you, not because they don't want whatever it is that you are selling.

#3 - Customer Service

Successful businesses go to great lengths to keep their customers happy. They understand that there is a high cost in obtaining new customers, and a relatively low cost in keeping existing customers. In a marketing survey conducted by A.T.&T. a few years ago, the company asked customers why they stopped doing business with the company. The results of the study were enlightening:

- 1% had died (an acceptable excuse not to buy!)
- 3% had moved out of the area in which the company did business
- 24% had a bad experience with the product or company
- 30% preferred doing business with another company for other reasons.
- 42% just felt "no one cared" about them.

As many as 96% of the customers lost could have been retained with more attention to customer relations! In a companion study, A.T.&T. compared marketing costs of obtaining a new customer with the expense of maintaining good relations to retain existing customers. That survey showed the cost ratio to be 9:1. For every ninety cents spent to obtain a new customer, they only needed to spend a dime to keep an existing one!

Also keep in mind that beyond the loss of one customer is the loss of the referral business that a satisfied customer could bring to the company (don't ever be bashful about asking for referrals!).

Q.L. Snook, founder of the Thomas Jefferson Life Insurance Company of America, raised four million dollars of investment capital before his company ever sold a single insurance policy. He decided that rather than go the usual route of raising capital from a few well-heeled investors, he would solicit funding from many smaller investors who, he reasoned, would also buy life insurance policies from the new company because of their vested interest as shareholders in seeing the company succeed. The fledgling company eventually raised four million dollars from more than seven thousand investors. Surprisingly, the investors were all derived from referrals generated by a small database that Snook and his co-founders skillfully developed. Each of the investors was asked to provide the names of five friends who might be interested in life insurance, then make initial contacts and schedule sales appointments. All that the company's salesmen had to do was to show up at the prescribed time, close the sale, and ask for another five names.

The process, to be successful, does require one important thing: the customer must be satisfied. Only then can you ask for, and expect to receive, referrals.

#4 - Customer Measurement

Relationship marketing specialists have an almost obsessive concern with measuring and collecting customers' personal data, which is then analyzed for such parameters as shifts in demand or preferences. A variety of sophisticated data-gathering techniques can be used, but the most common and effective is still one-on-one communication between the company and its customers. Too often, companies pay a high price to obtain customers, and then let them slip away because they do little or no follow-up communication and analysis. As part of the customer service function, ask questions such as: How is our product or service performing? How is our overall quality and workmanship? Is there anything you can suggest to improve our products or service? The last question is particularly important, because you are giving the customer an opportunity to give feedback. Don't forget that we are living in an "interactive" age, and communication should be two-way so that the relationship you are building is also two-way. A word of caution is in order here: your database is proprietary and confidential, and should be guarded carefully. If other companies or individuals obtain your database and use it for their own purposes, you could not only provide competitors with your valuable data, but you could also risk alienating your customers or violating privacy laws.

Customers and clients are generally willing to provide feedback, if you ask for it. Build a relationship and that customer will be a valuable asset to you in other ways than simply buying your products - there isn't much competition when it comes to exceptional follow-up service!

Measuring customer satisfaction after the sale can yield huge benefits, and as I've said before, it is far less expensive to retain present customers by keeping them satisfied than finding new customers. Continual monitoring of customers over long periods of time is unusual, and if you do it, you will surely stand head and shoulders above your competition.

#5 - Collaboration

Customer collaboration means that you and your customers move beyond the traditional adversarial seller/buyer relationship where you, the seller, want to receive the highest price for your product or service in every sale, and the buyer wants to pay the least amount possible. The idea is to turn this inherently adversarial relationship into a win-win situation by seeking a mutual benefit in every transaction.

So collaboration takes two separate paths, both equally important in building a solid relationship marketing program for your company. The first encompasses the benefits to your customer. Your goal is to satisfy a need or want for your customer, thus encouraging him or her to maintain a continuing business relationship with you, because he or she realizes a significant benefit when dealing with you. This requires a great deal of flexibility to accommodate a wide variety of customers, but ultimately, the effort will pay handsome returns.

The second path of collaboration is for your benefit. Once your client sees how valuable the relationship is to him or her, you can ask for not only additional business, but also a return flow of information. Because your business is more than likely not competing directly with your customers, they will not see you as a threat to them, and they will openly support the flow of shared information. If you are dealing with a client who is, or could be, a competitor, be sensitive to this, so that it doesn't appear as though you are asking for information that later could be used competitively against him.

#6 - Control

PLATO IS REMEMBERED THOUSANDS OF YEARS LATER AS ONE OF THE MOST WISE WESTERN PHILOSOPHERS.

Plato said that "knowledge is the ultimate weapon," and I think that is certainly true in relationship marketing. Keeping track of customers through in-depth communication and data gathering puts you in an enviable position: you know your customer better than he knows you, and when one party in any type of negotiation has superior knowledge, that party is in a better position to control the outcome. Yes, knowledge is indeed power.

Of course, if you have a client database of hundreds or thousands of names, it is usually impossible to remember a particular individual's personal information at a moment's notice. As your database grows, so does the need for a system for the gathering, storage and instantaneous retrieval of information. Later, I will discuss technology that will give you this capability.

#7 - Consistency

Building a solid relationship marketing/personal branding program means consistent follow-through with your clients, week after week, month after month, year after year. Even when you think that clients are not going to buy your product or service, you should keep them in your contact program. They may become buyers in the future, and you want them to think of you at that time. They probably also know people who may become buyers, and who they may refer to you. By being involved in your clients' lives, you may have the opportunity to solicit those people, and start the relationship-building process with them as new prospects.

Consistency also applies to the periodic measuring of your clients' buying habits, and what they think of you and your product offerings. If you carry this out unobtrusively, and cater to their wants and needs, when clients are ready to buy, they will most likely come to you.

Branding, or brand recognition, is built on consistency. Your product brand, or your personal brand, is essentially a "relationship" with your customers. It is an implied promise that your name represents quality and consistency, and that you stand behind your brand. It isn't just a logo, slogan, or name, because these are meaningless if they don't communicate the brand's promise of quality and reliability.

Whereas communication of a product's physical specifications like size, color, or style is straightforward and fast, communication of the value behind the brand is inherently circuitous and slow, requiring consistency and time to develop. Like an individual's character, the character of a brand is difficult to communicate. An individual cannot just come out and tell you what his or her character is. You must figure it out for yourself through a process that requires time and consistency. Unlike describing a product's physical attributes, which can simply be accomplished through print or media advertising, the character of your brand, like the character of a person, is defined as it matures over time.

Taking this short test will demonstrate the effectiveness of successful branding (fill in the blanks):

1   _____ tastes good, like a cigarette should.

2   I'd like to buy the world a _____.

3   I'd walk a mile for a _____.

4   Flick your _____.

5   Just do it! (company name -_____).

6   A _____ is forever.

(Answers: Winston, Coke, Camel, Bic, Nike, diamond).

One did not create brand recognition, as in these examples, with one 30-second commercial. It cost millions of dollars, and took many years of consistent, repeated exposure, for the brand names to be burned into our subconscious, so that even years after the promotions ended, we can instantly fill in the blanks. Yet, in spite of recognizing this phenomenon, many companies abandon the brand-building process because they don't really understand it, or it takes too long, or it's too difficult to measure, or requires too much of an investment.

Like product branding and Personal Branding, successful relationship marketing requires an investment of time, effort, and money. You need time to develop meaningful and beneficial relationships.

#8 - Communication

Communication is the key to building trust in personal relationships, and it forms the foundation for successful relationship marketing and Personal Branding as well. Your customers will appreciate your efforts. Even if your communication is merely a Christmas card once a year, it is more than most companies do to stay in touch. However, to be really effective, your efforts need to be substantially greater. Make it a goal to have some sort of contact with your clients at least once a month. It can take several forms, which I'll discuss later, but if at all possible, make it a personal call or visit, especially for your best clients. If that's not practical, use such things as newsletters, business letters, special offers and sales, and contests.

Communication with your customers should go beyond a simple "How are you? Do you need anything?" Relationship marketing, to be successful, must gather a broad range of information from clients, information that is needed to serve them better, and gain valuable insights, on a micro level, as to their lives and businesses, and on a macro level, as to trends in the overall market. Since two-way communication is necessary, information must also be given to the client as well, such as product developments, changes in the economy, and how these changes affect the client's life and/or business.

#9 - Chains of Relationships

One of the most important aspects of relationship marketing and Personal Branding is the link that is created between you, your business and a multitude of other businesses that are connected with your client. You may not even be aware of many of these links, because while your and your client's spheres of influence often

87

overlap, you may not be part of the overlap. However, the links are there, and may become apparent as you meet new acquaintances and explore mutual interests and relationships. Part of the complexity of a relationship marketing program is in the management of this entire chain of overlapping relationships, which may include business owners, management, directors, employees, investors, suppliers, bankers, labor unions, the media, etc. Don't be shy about asking questions, looking for overlapping interests, and exploiting them to mutual advantage.

#10 - Categorization

Categorization is important in defining the scope of products and services that are offered by your company, and the most efficient way to promote them. Because you should always tailor your products and services to meet customers' specific needs and desires as much as possible, if you have a large, diverse customer base, it will be necessary to develop a mass customization plan in which existing and new clients can all be serviced. This allows you to micro-manage a large variety of product offerings so that the right product goes to the right market segment.

Here is a summary of the ten "C's" of relationship marketing programs, all of which are indispensable and interrelated:

1   Customers / clients - define the focus of your efforts.
2   Contacts - creates the interface between your company and your customers, and opens vital lines of communication.
3   Customer service - the manner in which you relate to your customers.
4   Customer measurement - defines the parameters of your customer base.

5 Collaboration - defines the way mutual benefits are created from customer relationships.

6 Control - defines the manner and degree to which desired outcomes can be achieved.

7 Consistency - defines the time and effort needed to create successful relationships.

8 Communication - defines the effectiveness of the flow of information between you and your customers.

9 Chains - defines the way your business expands as you relate to an ever-expanding customer base.

10 Categorization - defines the scope of products and services to be offered.

"There are no such things as 'hard sell' and 'soft sell.' There is only 'smart sell' and 'stupid sell.' "
- Leo Burnett

❧ Chapter Four ❧
Learning From Others – Success Case Studies

The Ryder Company
In the mid-1980s, Ryder Systems, Inc. entered into a business relationship with one of the Bell telephone companies via a short-term truck rental agreement. Ryder's plan was to build the relationship by giving more value to the Bell Company than was typical in the industry at the time. Ryder provided the phone company not only with truck leases, but drivers, an outbound delivery system, and logistical solutions. They also assumed operation of all inbound transportation and distribution-center packaging, shipping, and cross docking and storeroom operations, all of which were staffed and operated by Ryder-supplied personnel. From a simple truck rental agreement, the account grew into a totally integrated supply-chain system worth more than $30 million annually to Ryder.

Building on an established customer relationship proved to be a powerful and efficient way for Ryder to grow. Their willingness to provide exceptional value to their customers and customized to their needs enabled both companies to grow stronger and more competitive.

"For us, relationship marketing is a question of survival," says Jerry Bowman, Ryder senior vice president. "The cost of securing new customers in this industry is very disagreeable. It's not unusual for a request-for-proposal response to a major client to cost us $250,000 to $500,000, due to the engineering work and the hours required to digest data and process the mountains of information. You can cost-of-sales yourself right out of business pretty quickly unless you're booking 80% of those proposals. It's much more cost-effective for us to pursue a major opportunity with a current client - plus, the returns on growth of existing accounts exceeds the returns we get selling business to a new client."

In this example, Ryder treated the customer relationship itself as an asset that could be evaluated and managed as rigorously as more traditional financial or physical assets. Go through your customer base and look for ways to develop your relationships with each customer. You've already done the expensive and difficult part in getting the customer in the first place - expanding along mutually beneficial lines to improve performance for both parties is clearly easier and more cost-effective than finding new customers.

So, the relationship becomes the central asset, not the customer. Customers are like unpolished gems. They have value in their raw state, but if shaped and polished, their value is greatly enhanced. The overall value of a company is ultimately equal to the sum of the values of its relationships with its customers. As in the Ryder example, a company can maximize the value of its customer relationships by helping its customers acquire, develop, and retain business. This thinking is different from the "product driven" sales development strategies of most companies. By building on relationships already in place, growth is generated internally.

Not all customers are good candidates for this approach, however, and like everything else in business, you should allocate time and resources where they will be most productive and efficient. To avoid spending too much of your valuable resources on those customer relationships which will likely not develop beyond a basic buy-sell transaction, these strategies must be applied selectively. You must develop a selection process to choose which companies you should manage as in the Ryder example, and which ones you are going to continue to service using traditional methods.

SQUARE D MANUFACTURING

The Square D Manufacturing Company, a major producer of electrical distribution, automation, and control products, illustrates an example of selective relationship building. Implementing a plan to build expanded relationships with its most profitable customers, Square D selected 200 key accounts from its customer base of 4,200. They transferred the servicing of the other 4,000 customers to their distributors. Square D then devoted greater effort towards improving the quality of its distributors, so that customer satisfaction was not compromised. Jack Carlson, vice president of Square D, called those 4,000 customers "transition accounts." The distributors thus became "key strategic assets, and have allowed us to focus our resources on our key OEM accounts, which are down to about 200 right now, from the 4,200 of just a year ago." It's not uncommon for a few key accounts to comprise the bulk of a company's business, and by nurturing those accounts, greater sales growth can be achieved than by spreading limited resources too thin in trying to service every account, no matter how insignificant it may be in the overall mix.

The top 200 accounts comprised more than 40% of the company's business. With strategic and coordinated planning, Square D increased sales from these 200 accounts by over 40% during the first year of the program. While the results of the program were impressive from a sales growth perspective, they were absolutely stunning on the expense side, having reduced operating costs by 30%. Square D was servicing fewer customers, had cut operating costs by 30%, and had a level of customer satisfaction unequaled in the history of the company.

"When we first started this program, we were all very nervous," says Carlson. "There is a lot of archaic thinking out there, and frankly, we didn't know whether our target 200 would be receptive to new ideas, or resist change, thinking we were after something. We've invested heavily into the operations of our target 200, but the returns were almost immediate. With strong relationships going into an operation like this, you don't have to overcome that hurdle."

Instead of the adversarial relationship that is customary between buyers and sellers, Square D opened a flow of communication between themselves and their targeted 200 customers. No area of cooperation was overlooked. Square D and its customers integrated functions wherever possible, delved into each other's operations on a function-by-function basis, established joint marketing and product development programs, and even consolidated manufacturing facilities in several instances.

Carlson characterized meetings with the target 200 as "being difficult to tell who is the customer and who is the supplier. We perceive each relationship as a relationship between someone inside our company and an individual and function on a corresponding side inside their company."

To illustrate an example of the success of Square D's efforts, consider the Trane Company, one of Square D's target 200 clients.

"Part of our expanded relationship with Trane includes guaranteed price reductions every year, which they were overjoyed to accept, but at the same time they agreed to open doors for us with sister companies under the American Standard Companies (Trane's parent company) umbrella," says Carlson. "That account has grown from about $1 million when we first started the

94

relationship marketing effort to well more than $10 million in the last three years, with no end in sight."

Trane engineers participate on selected Square D development teams, and Square D has developed and manufactured PC boards for Trane. While foregoing replacement sales, Square D gained access to more than $2 million worth of new products that they had been locked out of before. The two companies continue to work together with other related companies, and have formed a consortium to leverage their buying power with other companies, such as United Air Lines and American Express.

"It's given us a whole new perspective on our industry," Carlson concludes. "We never could have imagined working on a business like American Express in the past. Now, we realize that if one of our target 200 accounts can land the business, we've landed the business as well."

In modern parlance, this is a good example of a strategic alliance.

PROCTOR & GAMBLE COMPANY

In 1997, the Proctor and Gamble Company embraced the concept of partnering, or forming strategic alliances, with its customers and renamed its worldwide sales organization "Customer Business Development." While competitors saw this as merely a cosmetic change, and took little notice of it, "this was a watershed change in how Proctor and Gamble took its brands to market," said Lawrence Milligan, senior vice president of customer business development. "Simply put, to deliver greater customer value, we moved from a tactical focus upon short-term merchandising to a strategic and systemic cooperation with our customers."

P&G also reduced the size of their product lines and price promotions in a move designed to save $1.35 billion between 1997 and 2000. P&G lowered its costs and slowed the frantic race for a larger and larger customer base, and they have begun to refocus their efforts on mutually beneficial promotions and operations with their best customers. Although secretive about the details of their proprietary consumer research, P&G has openly replaced traditional sales reps with multi-functional teams in areas of market research, finance, logistics, shelf management, sales/marketing, and manufacturing. Links with major retail P&G accounts now include logistics and systems coordination, joint activity-based costing, standardization of databases and common analytical tools.

Milligan summarizes the transition from a concentrated effort to develop new customers and product lines, to a focus on increased development of business from current customers as follows:

"Think systemically, not transactionally. Anyone can, and will, beat you on price. To think systemically, you must be multi-functional and involve both buyer and seller in planning. Multi-functional customer teams need leaders who can sell, not necessarily established sales people trying to lead. Simplify and standardize first. Don't mechanize complexity."

Many companies, including Ryder, Square D, and Proctor and Gamble, are building value with current customers by expanding product and service offerings. They are offering their size, experience and resources to their customers to be utilized as an extension of the customer's company. It's a win-win situation for everyone involved.

Many other companies have shared resources for mutually beneficial results.

Federal Express teamed up with one of its customers, Bay Networks, Inc., a computer network products company. FedEx allowed Bay Networks' customers to drop PC parts in any of the numerous FedEx warehouses worldwide. In return for the rapid turnaround and convenience to Bay Networks' customers, Bay has given FedEx all of their PC-board shipping business. Cycle time for Bay Networks was cut from 21 days to five days, and FedEx received significant additional business.

Grainger Inc., an industrial distribution firm, recently orchestrated a new operation that works in partnership with its vendors. In a single contract with American Airlines, the company saved American $500,000 on $2 million worth of business in one year via inventory optimization, product consolidation and cost savings expertise.

Coca-Cola matches its sales reps' expertise to their customers' business needs. As an example, an operations-oriented team served a customer who was opening new outlets, and a marketing-oriented team served the same customer in redesigning that customer's brand.

I've used these few examples to illustrate that relationship marketing and related Personal Branding programs mean much more than simply "doing business with a friend." The processes involved can be complex and innovative. Relationship marketing managers think differently than traditional marketing managers. Their strategy is proactive, designed to achieve diverse and possibly wide-ranging benefits for both the company and its customers, and the process can become very involved. It boils down to asking not "how can I entice people to buy my product or service?" but "how can I assist my customers to achieve their goals, and possibly use my products or service in the process?"

This shift in thinking involves elements of selecting, identifying, delivering and evaluating.

As in the Square D Manufacturing or the Proctor and Gamble examples, the process begins by selecting a specific and quantitative target market. This doesn't mean that you should discontinue servicing your non-targeted customer base, but rather that you should focus your efforts on a core target group of clients,

97

or even prospective clients, to whom you will aim your relationship-marketing program. This group might be the top 10% of your client list, as was the case in the Square D Manufacturing strategy. Or, it may be a geographical area, a certain income level of your client base, an age bracket, or even a special group of clients whom you believe would most appreciate your efforts. The goal is to generate additional business from within your current customer mix, rather than focusing your energy and resources on gaining new customers.

Your objective is to invest a good deal of strategic planning and experimentation in the direction of these select clients. Thus, you want them to be top-quality clients, to reduce the risk of insignificant returns for your efforts.

THE SECOND ASPECT of the process is identifying your selected market and designing specific messages to deliver to it. The message should be custom-designed, tailored to meet the specific needs of your target client. That doesn't mean that every message you select needs to be unique for each client. Indeed, it may be the same message for more than one, or even all, of your selected audience.

The right message must offer a significant benefit to the clients you've selected. Be careful not to create the impression that this is just another sales call to push your product. For example, you may personally visit selected clients with the stated purpose of defining their needs, and carefully integrate your message into the conversation.

(The synergy created by friendly relations among competitors can also be a benefit to all. For example, the local Association of Realtors® in any community is comprised of competitors, yet through the association, every member benefits).

Your message is analogous to the platform of a political candidate. If you send the wrong or a confusing message to your clients, the process may end before it has a chance to begin. Like the political candidate, you should respond to your voters' (clients') needs to get their "vote." Design your message around these types of questions:

- What does my client need?
- What do I have that my clients want?
- What are my clients' greatest problems, and how may I help to solve them?
- How can I become more valuable to my clients than my competitors are?
- How can I increase their dependence on me?

Just as the political candidate makes campaign promises that are designed to garner votes from his or her constituency (target market), so must your message be compelling enough and beneficial enough to provoke a positive response from your customers, clients, and prospects. Think through your message, articulate it, sculpt and design it, just as a writer would sculpt a poem or a page in a book.

In the Square D Manufacturing example, the company lowered prices to their target client, Trane Air Conditioning. That certainly got Trane's attention. In return, Square D asked for Trane's vendor list, and both companies profited from their cooperation.

Federal Express wanted Bay Networks' PC-board business and offered Bay access to their worldwide drop system, allowing Bay Networks' customers the ease of using certain FedEx drop stations. The benefit to Bay Networks was greater customer service with a faster turnaround time, while FedEx benefited by expanding their business relationship with Bay Networks. In this instance, the message that FedEx sent to Bay Networks wasn't based on cost savings, but time savings, and a way for Bay to improve service to their customers.

In both cases, business relationships with existing customers were strengthened, and grew as a result of strategic planning and identifying the right message for the particular client.

Following are a few questions to ask yourself to test important components of your message:

- Does it help build your customer's profitability?
- Does it "customize" your product or service to your clients, tailoring it to their particular needs?
- Does it promote enthusiasm and cooperation between you and your clients?
- Does it build your company's image and enhance awareness of its products among your customers?
- Does the message promote ongoing dialog and communication with your clients?
- Will it improve customer loyalty?
- Will the plan create more business for both you and your clients?
- Is the message workable? Is it succinct enough to be effective?

Suppose you target a major client on your select list. You want your message to convey a significant benefit, so you first seek to identify your client's most important needs. You also try to anticipate the barriers that your client may perceive which could impede the acceptance of your message (often called "objections"), and prepare to remove these barriers if your client brings them up. As an example, suppose your client is an active supporter of the Boy Scouts in your community. Rather than approach the client through a traditional sales cold call, you offer to let the Scouts use a facility that you own that is perfect for their meetings, and through your offer, you gain access to your target client. While this example is rather simplistic, it illustrates the point - select your target client, identify a mutually beneficial message, and deliver it so as to maximize the chance of its acceptance.

THE THIRD INGREDIENT is delivery. Here is where relationship marketing and/or Personal Branding really set themselves apart from traditional sales approaches, which have mainly utilized the media. But as I have already pointed out, advertising on a local radio station or in the newspaper is much less effective today than it was in the past, before today's massive onslaught of advertising dulled the listener's or reader's attention span. It is increasingly expensive and inefficient to disseminate your message in this manner. If you must use a traditional medium, try to identify the most targeted medium in your particular area or for your particular product line (remember that the surest method of delivery is still via a personal call). But you should not use a shotgun approach here in any case, because we are interested in building one-on-one relationships. Square D Manufacturing didn't design a plan for Trane Air Conditioning and then run a newspaper ad to bring it to their attention. Square D called them, arranged for a meeting and delivered the message in person.

Target the right market with the right message in the right medium and you can expect exceptional results.

THE FOURTH AND FINAL INGREDIENT is evaluation. Evaluating the results of your efforts to your target market is critical in any marketing effort. Surprisingly, very few companies really examine the results they are obtaining. If they did, I'm sure they would be upset by the meager 2%-3% return on their investment! Wouldn't it be great if they could avoid the 97%-98% waste? If your $480 newspaper ad yielded ten calls and one $500 sale, wouldn't you consider the campaign a failure? Small companies especially often don't carefully plan and evaluate the process of delivering their messages, and they spend little, if any, time evaluating the results.

Evaluation tells you many things. It identifies shortcomings of your strategy, and it details the costs and benefits. Evaluation also shows your clients that you care enough to ask how the program benefits them and that you are anxious to correct shortcomings, if any.

Major media advertising isn't terribly effective primarily because you are often going after the wrong audience! Focus on building relationships that yield better results for both parties, rather than merely shot gunning for new customers.

"You can't wait for the phone to ring.
You have to ring them."
- Lord Lew Grade

❧ **Chapter Five** ❧

Loyalty Magic™

THERE IS A VERITABLE ARSENAL of techniques and strategies being successfully employed by relationship marketers. Your task is to identify the techniques that work best in your particular situation, and get your own program started.

Following are several categories of strategies to consider:

1) Loyalty Magic™
   a) Recognition programs - clubs and cards
   b) Rewards programs

2) AutoMagic Marketing™
   a) Automated e-mail correspondence and interactive voice response
   b) Maximizing the power of your computer
   c) Using the Internet to build your business

3) Effectively using the mainstream media
   a) Pros and cons of using the media
   b) Low-cost media opportunities

4) Building the Brand of Choice
   a) The importance of your name
   b) Branding vs. Promotion
   c) Branding tips that can change your business

5) Becoming a local celebrity
   a) Tips on using the media
   b) Seminars and consulting
   c) Public speaking
   d) Becoming an author

6) Reciprocity and Response Marketing
   a) The "rule of fives" in referrals
   b) Golden Rule marketing
   c) Powerful giving

7) Power networking
   a) Networking tips

LOYALTY MAGIC™

As you know, it's much more expensive to obtain a new customer than it is to keep one - or to reactivate an old one who no longer does business with you - and it amazes me that so many companies still seem to prefer chasing after new customers to make a first sale rather than staying in touch with old customers for repeat business! Consider a satisfied customer to be like a perennial flower in your garden - with proper care, you can usually count on it to bloom year after year. It is less expensive, and more satisfying, to

Loyalty

simply nurture the plant you've got than dig it out every year, buy another, plant it and care for it until it reaches maturity and blooms.

Compare your new customer with a tomato seed. Planted and cared for, the seed will germinate and grow into a tomato plant. As the plant grows, it blooms, and perhaps bears ten tomatoes. These ten tomatoes might be compared with ten new prospects that your satisfied customer or client introduces to you. The ten tomatoes all contain seeds - more than one hundred seeds each! Ten tomatoes yield a thousand seeds. One thousand seeds could grow into a thousand plants, and a thousand plants could yield a hundred thousand more seeds! What an incredible return on your investment in one seed (or satisfied customer)! Satisfied, loyal customers are the most valuable assets your firm can have.

The benefits of a planned loyalty-building program can be extraordinary. Recently, the property manager of a large newly-renovated apartment complex in Orlando, Florida, determined that advertising in four publications, and the occasional use of radio spots and direct mail cost her company $540 to generate each one-year lease. She prepared a flier and sent it to each of her existing tenants. She offered every resident $100 worth of free groceries for every referral that signed a one-year lease. During the first three weeks of the promotion, the property manager received more than one hundred referrals per week. She leased sixty units, and quickly filled the complex. She went one step further, and negotiated a ten percent volume discount with a local supermarket.

She not only saved her company more than $12,000 in advertising dollars, but more significantly, she built loyalty with the residents who became her most valuable source of new tenant referrals whenever there was a vacancy. She now manages fourteen properties for the parent company and continues to use similar loyalty-building promotions to fill periodic vacancies.

When a customer buys your service or product for the first time, he or she is casting a vote of confidence in you and your offering.

This is not just a "sale," but also the start of a potentially longer-term relationship. Do not consider a sale just selling somebody something; you are building satisfaction and loyalty, and hopefully, obtaining a customer for life.

As we have seen in previous chapters, staying in touch with your customers is certainly important, but offering them a tailored, exclusive benefit is how true loyalty is built. How do you know what your customers and clients need or want? The easiest way to find out is just to ask them.

An upscale men's clothier in New Orleans knows that his pricey suits aren't for everyone, and he has always maintained a rather "exclusive" air about his business. When contacted by an advertising sales rep from the local newspaper, the clothier informed him that he never advertised in the media.

"How do you get new customers then?" the inquisitive rep asked.

"I have all the new customers I can handle," the clothier replied.

"Without advertising?"

"No, I advertise through my past clients. For each new customer they refer to me, I send them a $100 gift certificate. At Christmas, I give all of my customers free tickets to see The Nutcracker. I have all the new customers that I can handle."

The actual out-of-pocket expense for this retailer to obtain a new customer was less than $50 each. The tailor asked each new customer to complete a short questionnaire when they made their first purchase, asking such personal information as birth dates, anniversary dates, ages of children, even the names of household pets. On each birthday or significant anniversary, he sent a personal card with a free-lunch gift certificate to the customer. Do you think this businessman has a loyal customer base?

A florist in Chicago maintains a database of the special occasions for every purchase made by her customers (the store clerk merely asks the customer for this information at the time of purchase). Ten days prior to anniversaries and birthdays, the florist mails a postcard, sends an e-mail, or telephones the customers to remind them of their event, and tells them that a dozen roses (or whatever they last purchased) has been reserved for them. Customers never forget an anniversary, and sales have skyrocketed.

In this increasingly impersonal world, every personal touch adds strength to a customer relationship that no amount of price discounting from a competitor can overcome. It isn't difficult to come up with innovative ideas. Ask yourself a few key questions such as these:

- What do my customers want and need that I can provide?
- Can I offer something that is mutually beneficial?
- Am I promoting loyalty?
- Does it "customize" my product or service, tailoring it to the needs of my customers?
- Does it build my company's image and enhance awareness of my products in the marketplace?
- Does it promote ongoing communication with my customers and clients?
- Is it workable? Will it be effective and manageable?

Let's look at another example. A real estate agent in Tampa, Florida grows pumpkins. Every fall, his five-acre pumpkin patch yields hundreds of pumpkins, which is more than he can sell, and they are left to rot in his field. One day, he had a great idea: he decided to deliver free pumpkins to all of his clients. He hired a driver and using his own truck, he surprised his clients with a free Halloween pumpkin delivered right to their homes.

The agent's clients were impressed that he thought so highly of them and they swamped him with thank-you cards and phone calls. There was little doubt about the success of his program, so the Realtor® expanded his pumpkin giveaway to include all the homeowners in his geographic "farm area." Many surprised homeowners called to thank him for this unexpected gift and the agent soon became the dominant listing agent in his area. Then the agent got the biggest surprise of all. One of the houses that he had delivered a pumpkin to was the home of a reporter for the local newspaper. A front-page story with a full-color photo of the agent delivering pumpkins hit the streets a week later. He became known affectionately as "The Pumpkin Man." Do you think he has prospered because of his relationship-marketing approach to listing properties? Pumpkins alone didn't do the job, of course - he is also a very competent real estate agent. But the pumpkin giveaway set him apart from the crowd, gave him a distinctive face, and endeared him to clients jaded after years of impersonal sales approaches.

Simply "staying in touch" with your customers isn't enough to build lasting loyalty. Relationship marketing and building a personal brand aren't just about saying "hello" to your clients at a cocktail party every now and then, or calling them once a month. The relationship must go to a deeper level than that. As a start, learn to do some simple things:

NAME NAMES. I have already stated that in today's world of account numbers, nothing is more impressive than individual, personalized attention. There is no more appreciated sound in the world of commerce than that of a person's own name. One of the key elements in building loyalty with your customers is to put away their account numbers and use their names!

CUSTOM CARE. Customers know what they want and don't want from you and your business. If you never ask them what they want, you'll never know. If you don't write the information down, you'll forget it, and if you don't use the data, the whole exercise is a waste of time. Remembering valuable information about your customers and making good use of that knowledge, is another key element in relationship marketing.

KEEPING IN TOUCH. You have to communicate on a one-to-one basis with your customers (without becoming a pest). This means no pushy "sales calls", no high pressure selling; it means that you have listened to and understood them, and delivered what they want. Here's an example: if you see a newspaper article pertaining to your customers' business or personal life, clip it and send it to them, letting them know you're thinking about them. When customers know you've taken time out of your busy day to think about them, they won't soon forget you.

"OOPS" RESEARCH. Part of every successful loyalty program is taking the time to find out why your customers chose to do business with someone other than you. In many cases, just making contact to let them know that you care, and value their business, is enough to win them back. Ask them why they left, and perhaps you can learn an important lesson about what you may be doing wrong, and not only get them back as customers, but avoid losing others.

JOIN THE CLUB

Loyalty clubs and organizations have been around for a long time, but business was slow to pick up on their real value and purpose until fairly recently. One of the best known and largest of these organizations is the American Association of Retired Persons (AARP), founded in 1958 by retired educator, Dr. Ethel Percy Andrus. By 1999, AARP's membership stood at approximately thirty million, and is expected to almost double in size as more and more "baby boomers" reach the age of 50 over the next few years. The American Automobile Association (AAA) is another very successful loyalty organization with more than fifteen million members.

Both of these organizations were originally underwritten by insurance companies as a way of selling insurance through the concurrent offering of club benefits. The branding of these "clubs" is so effective that when people think of automobile travel, they think of AAA, and when they contemplate retirement, it is AARP that comes to mind.

The idea of "joining a club" is attractive to many people because it fosters a sense of belonging. Economically driven clubs such as AARP and AAA offer such benefits as free magazines, discounted insurance rates, consumer information, discounts in related and associated joint ventures with other companies, and advice. There may be a nominal fee to join, which is designed more to weed out unmotivated people and cover the cost of the membership paperwork, but the real economic benefit to the organization comes from sale of the other goods and services purchased by members, and from shared benefits with affiliated providers.

Loyalty clubs generate billions of dollars in sales and involve every segment of the economy, including banking, retailing, manufacturing, wholesaling, travel, retirement and hobbies. A recent study conducted by the Commerce Department found that Americans carry an average of 4.5 club cards, including movie clubs, frequent flyer clubs, fitness clubs, bank clubs, hotel clubs, social clubs, restaurant clubs, coffee clubs, grocery store clubs....

What does all of this mean to you and your business? It means that if you're not utilizing loyalty clubs, you are missing out on a potentially lucrative way to retain customers and generate significant repeat business. Clubs can be designed for virtually any business. Just be sure to offer benefits sufficient in value to motivate members to pay any fees you may charge to join or maintain club membership, or to expend any effort required to participate.

Clubs offer an unobtrusive way to communicate frequently with your customers. It's a good idea to send monthly newsletters, offering additional membership benefits so that you are not only communicating with your customers, but you are giving them something new to keep their interest alive. You never stop selling but by using this method, you avoid badgering your customers for the sale. They buy because the sale is part of a wider club benefit.

An enterprising real estate broker in Phoenix, Arizona wanted to start a club to get a competitive edge in obtaining listings, as well as to develop a means of keeping in touch with his many clients. The broker went to several other businesses in his area and formed alliances, and each offered a free or discounted service, such as a low-cost oil change, two-for-one meals, free or discounted merchandise, and a host of other benefits. There was no membership fee, and the club benefits were worth hundreds of dollars. Only the most skeptical would refuse to join a club that offered such valuable benefits, with no strings attached. The broker tripled his listings in the first year that he offered his club. The filled-out applications gave him all the information he needed to build a detailed database that enabled him to communicate with his clients on the important days of their lives such as birthdays and anniversaries, as well as a way to keep track of their address changes. His idea evolved into a major real estate firm's "Consumer Card," which now has membership in the thousands, offering a travel club, singles group, discounted group health insurance, and of course, all the real estate information any member could ever want.

The loyalty club, by its nature, isn't really designed for prospective customers. It is designed for your current customers, enhancing communication and offering special deals for those who participate (obviously, it can also be a potent prospecting tool, since non-customers will want to sign up for the benefits). Once the club is formed, it is relatively easy to create innovative ways to set up mutually advantageous cooperative ventures with other businesses, and thus, as an added benefit you establish valuable alliances with those other businesses. It is a triple win: a win for the customer, a win for your business, and a win for the other businesses in your coalition. Consider forming alliances with other welcome clubs as well. Many have extensive databases and have done considerable research that could be of great value to you.

As with any complex undertaking, developing a loyalty club requires planning. The following steps may prove helpful and get you off to a successful start, rather than an expensive blunder.

Loyalty-Magic™ Step One

Analyze the situation carefully. Obtain a complete understanding of your customers' needs, wants and desires. The success of any loyalty club depends on its being beneficial to you and your customers. If they don't want what you offer, you won't be successful. You could conduct an informal market survey by polling your employees and friends to find out if what you plan to offer as benefits meets the minimum criterion of success, namely: do people really want what you are offering through your club? You may even wish to poll your customers, letting them know that you are forming an association that will offer some excellent benefits, with their needs in mind. Ask them in a brief questionnaire for their opinions of your proposed offerings, and anything additional that they would like to see. This not only gives you the feedback you need, but also builds interest and anticipation among your customers.

Remember to be innovative. Your goal is to be different, to stand out from the rest of the crowd. By their very nature, Personal Branding and relationship marketing are more proactive than the relatively passive approaches of the past, whereby a company would often ask a newspaper's advertising department to design ads for them, and then keep their fingers crossed that the ads bring in new business. You would be far better off to hire an advertising agency, and spend the money to have them design compelling advertising for you. Be aware, however, that relatively few ad agencies really understand relationship marketing, having the mind-set of a more traditional approach, and they are likely to design ad campaigns to sell, rather than motivate customers to seek you out because they like doing business with you. Always review your agency's work and don't be afraid to take exception if the results don't do the job to your satisfaction. Remember that ad agencies are businesses that need your account. A good ad agency will want to build a relationship with you and will therefore take a vested interest in the results of your advertising. You should pay particular attention to your ad program because many ad agencies will want to use mass media (TV, radio, newspapers) since they collect commissions and design fees that might contradict relationship marketing/Personal Branding benefits.

It will take some imagination to come up with the right program. First ask yourself the basic question, "What do my customers want and need that I can provide them?" Don't forget emotional needs and wants - don't focus only on the practical or financial. Keep in mind that some of the most successful loyalty clubs deal strictly with the dissemination of information. People need and want to be informed and they'll pay considerable amounts of money for information and advice. By taking the time to analyze, rather than guess at your customers' needs and wants, you'll find the right club format and design the right benefits. Ask the following questions:

Is your club beneficial to members? Smokescreens can and will be detected by club members very quickly. If the obvious purpose of your loyalty club is to generate sales for your company without offering something beneficial to your members, you will fail in your attempt, and you may simply create hard feelings toward your company. If you err, make it on the side of giving too much rather than too little.

Does your club promote loyalty to your business? If all you are doing through your club is offering your customers benefits provided by unrelated businesses, you may actually do very little to promote loyalty to yourself. You might actually be building loyalty between your customer and someone else's business. When that happens, you've accomplished nothing for your efforts, or worse, you may have delivered a customer to a competitor. Remember the goal of any loyalty club is to build loyalty - to you! For example, suppose you own a small video rental business and you need a compelling way to encourage customers to patronize your store rather than the large Blockbuster store across the street. So you arrange with a consumer electronics retailer to give your customers a free MP-3 player or DVD player when they have accumulated enough "points" by renting videos from your store. Obviously, it will take a lot of points to get the free player, but it is sufficient incentive to build loyalty to your business.

Does it "customize" your product or service, tailoring it to the needs of your customers? Merely copying other loyalty clubs doesn't do much to set you apart from your competition. Your club and its benefits must deliver your product to your customers in a way that they will appreciate and enjoy. Don't forget about your customer's associates, family and friends. You may design club benefits for your customers' children, for example. Be creative!

Does it build your or your company's image and enhance awareness? It takes a great deal of effort to build a brand and become a household word, or to create a unique identity if you are in a commodity-type business such as a hardware store, or a real estate office. Well-known multi-national companies such as McDonald's, Pepsi, Nike and others probably don't need to continue to advertise heavily to stay in business. So why do you think they do such things as spend millions of dollars on thirty-second Super Bowl commercials? They do so to stay on top of their businesses to strengthen their brand names and grow their market shares. For them, it isn't a matter of survival - it's a matter of continually enhancing their images and staying on top. Remember that the marketplace is fickle, and customers fall out of love easily. Don't neglect them!

Does it promote ongoing dialog and two-way communication with your customers? The goal of relationship marketing and Personal Branding is to have your customers call you at least as much as you call them (but not to complain, of course!). That's two-way communication. The loyalty club you design must enable and encourage that type of communication if you are to succeed in the long run. Offering free cappuccino in your lobby might be great for your customers, but does it promote ongoing communication? Unless you can use the gratuity to enhance dialog with your club members, you've probably given the wrong perk, and are not getting the full benefit from your effort.

Is it workable? Will it be effective and manageable? Before you commit yourself and your staff to a project such as a loyalty club, you need to answer this key question: Will the time, energy and expense required to get it off the ground be worth all the effort? Will it be manageable so that you can still perform all the other important functions that you currently perform? It may require additional staff, space or services. Be sure it's worth the expense and effort. And don't forget the ultimate purpose of your club. Do not allow it to become the end in itself. You're not in the club business!

Your loyalty club will most likely not be an overnight success, and it won't be accomplished without persistent effort. Successful relationship marketing and Personal Branding is a gradual thing, just like building personal relationships takes time.

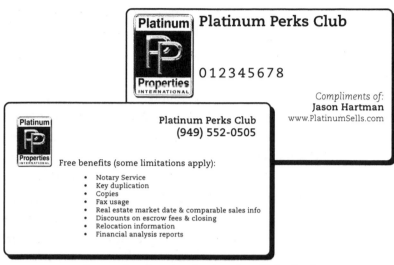

Platinum Perks Club

012345678

Compliments of:
Jason Hartman
www.PlatinumSells.com

Platinum Perks Club
(949) 552-0505

Free benefits (some limitations apply):

- Notary Service
- Key duplication
- Copies
- Fax usage
- Real estate market date & comparable sales info
- Discounts on escrow fees & closing
- Relocation information
- Financial analysis reports

Example of a simple Loyalty Club Card

Loyalty-Magic™ Step Two

Research your plan thoroughly before implementing it. A national health food chain created a popular nutrition and cooking club for its customers in the late 1980's. It became an immediate success and grew very quickly, expanding to local television where the cooking and nutrition show became a weekly morning "must-watch" for thousands of viewers. Memberships were offered at the conclusion of the show, and the numbers of club members grew exponentially. All was sailing along smoothly until the CEO of the company received a complaint from a company claiming to own the trademark used by the loyalty club and cooking show. When the Ohio-based health food company researched the trademark, they confirmed that they were indeed infringing on the other company's trademark. The resulting settlement stipulated that the television show and the club must be closed or renamed. The company's attempts to rename the club and television show were handled as poorly as the original research, and in the confusion that followed, the momentum was lost, members quit, and the program failed. A successful idea had been torpedoed by sloppy planning and the company shot itself in the foot big time!

This is a good illustration of how loyalty clubs can become so popular that they can alter the course of a company's future, but if poorly administered, they can also damage or destroy it. The clubs often take on lives of their own. Be sure you are prepared to handle possibly explosive growth, and be sure you are able to afford the expenditure of time, energy and money that may be required to fuel and maintain the club's growth. If properly set up, your loyalty club can become one of your firm's most valuable relationship-building assets. However, you don't want the club to become the focus of your efforts, to the ultimate detriment of your core business. Don't let the tail wag the dog!

Before you launch your club, it is wise to research other loyalty programs that may be operated by businesses similar to yours, or which target the same prospective customer base. One way to gather information about the existence and success of other clubs is to include questions on the polling questionnaire that you use to gather data on your customers. Ask whether they belong to, or have considered clubs similar to the one you are planning. Ask them to describe their experience, and whether it has been a satisfactory one. If they considered joining a club, and decided not to, try to find out why not. Often, the reasons why someone else was unsuccessful is more helpful than the reasons why they succeeded. You can benefit from their mistakes!

Learn from the example I used above. Make sure that you thoroughly research the names, trademarks, slogans or logos of clubs and programs that you propose to launch. While you may be able to search trademarks, copyrights, and logos by yourself, in law libraries, or via the Internet, it is wise to have this type of research done professionally, just to be sure. Start by visiting the U.S. Patent and Trademark Office's website (www.uspto.gov) to do preliminary research on your trademark name ideas, and if you have difficulty, or are unsure of the availability of your trademark, you should hire an attorney to do a thorough search. This can be your best investment to avoid false starts or expensive mistakes during the early stages of your planning. If the name of your club has not already been trademarked or copyrighted, register your own claim to protect use of the name. This also avoids the possibility of someone else using and profiting from it, or preventing you from using it. An ounce of prevention is worth a pound of cure in this situation!

Loyalty-Magic™ Step Three

Set concise and well-defined objectives for your club using the goal-setting techniques already discussed. When setting your objectives, remember to ask the key relationship marketing questions, and find ways to answer them for the mutual benefit of you and your club members. You should also decide how best to disseminate your message to your customers.

Loyalty-Magic™ Step Four

Integrate your club into your entire organization. Once your club is up and running, it will not exist in a vacuum. It will become an integral part of your business and will probably have an impact on other company functions. How will the loyalty club interact with your business as a whole? How much should it interact, or shouldn't interact? What will be the time frame for the club - is it going to be permanent or only exist for a limited time? What will happen to the club after your initial goals are realized? You should develop a good exit strategy during the planning stage so that you can eventually wind down the club without leaving members feeling abandoned or betrayed. By developing specific objectives for the loyalty program, and by developing a broader set of objectives as to how the program will interact with your business overall, you will be able to maintain balance, avoiding the common mistake of investing too many resources into a calculated experiment, rather than managing the loyalty club as a part of the whole. You don't want the whole to be less than the sum of its parts!

Loyalty-Magic™ Step Five

Do a cost and benefit analysis. The overriding purpose of a loyalty program is to increase sales and profits for your company. Don't get sidetracked into spending your time and resources on issues unrelated to this purpose. Develop a budget that outlines all of the costs of the program, add 10-15% to the result for a safety margin, and analyze the benefits as it progresses. Do the benefits justify the costs? Are the benefits significant enough to attract and retain customers to your program? Also, guard against deterioration in the results. While the program may be profitable at lower levels, it may slip into the loss column as it grows. Administration, clerical, data collection, advertising, etc. costs can expand exponentially as the program takes root. Be sure you run the program - don't let it run you!

Loyalty-Magic™ Step Six

The next step is implementation of your plan. How are you going to start it, promote it, and interest people in joining it? What obstacles do you foresee? Make sure that you have a multiple delivery method. A simple mailing to your customers might not be sufficient to get the project off the ground. Because at first your program will be geared to existing customers, you probably will not be using newspapers, radio, or television, but there is no reason not to use the media if you determine that it will be effective.

Obviously, the time required to complete these six steps is in direct proportion to the magnitude and complexity of your loyalty program. Remember, you are building long-term customer relationships. Do not be tempted to shortcut the process. The potential payoff is great, but the risks of failure are high.

REWARD YOUR CUSTOMERS

Like loyalty clubs, reward programs are not new. One of the largest and most successful of the early reward programs was S&H Green Stamps, founded in the 1930's. By the early 1970's, almost one in every three American families was licking and sticking S&H Green Stamps into little stamp saving books. The program worked in typical loyalty reward fashion - participating businesses gave their customers Green Stamps for every purchase made with the number of stamps based on the dollar amount of the purchase. Stamps could be redeemed for merchandise that was selected from a special catalog. The number of stamps required for the item was indicated in the catalog.

The advent of large discount stores in the 1970's proved to be the death knell of Green Stamps, and they quickly disappeared from the scene. Rather than pay higher prices at traditional smaller stores, consumers stopped saving the stamps and opted instead for the lower prices and convenience of the large discount stores. But changing conditions in retailing did not blind perceptive marketing executives to the impact that well-designed reward programs can have if properly implemented.

Bonus cards and stamp programs still exist. They are particularly popular with grocery chains that now use some form of reward program for their customers. Rather than offer discounts to everyone who walks into the store, savings are given only to club members in the form of club card savings. You simply produce your card at checkout, and the savings are deducted from your bill.

As successful as these programs are in enhancing customer loyalty, however, many stores and other businesses such as restaurants do not maximize the potential of their reward/loyalty systems, even when they are actively engaged in using one. The programs offer a great opportunity to get to know customers and develop relationships by utilizing the information club members provide when they apply for the bonus cards, and by analyzing the consumption information which can be gathered by computers at the checkout stand. But many businesses find the process too involved and cumbersome, so they take the path of least resistance, and just use the card programs as if they were discount clubs. They miss the valuable opportunity to use the club to get to know their customers more thoroughly, and build meaningful relationships with them.

A wide range of businesses now uses reward systems. These systems exist in a variety of forms, but all of them have one feature in common - they reward their customers with discounts or free merchandise for their repeat business. Consumers have come to expect these savings programs from the merchants they patronize. This is especially true in frequent flier miles programs used by some airlines, and in grocery store clubs used to attract savings-conscious shoppers. Customers realize that they are a valuable asset for the business and expect some sort of recognition and appreciation from the merchant. If you don't have a rewards program in place at your business, now is the time to consider one.

When creating a rewards program, follow the same basic steps I previously outlined for loyalty clubs. Although simple bonus card programs can be implemented with less complexity and expense than more sophisticated clubs and associations, they must offer real value, or your customers will perceive your program as a mere come-on to sell them merchandise or services, and carrying your card will be more of a nuisance than a benefit. Such a perception must be avoided or the rewards program could have unintended negative consequences and do your customer relationships more harm than good. Another perception that must be avoided is that you have raised prices to offset the discount. Remember the golden rule of relationship marketing and Personal Branding - whatever you do, it must be sincere and mutually beneficial for you and your customers. Anything less will likely be perceived as a sales gimmick, and can undermine your efforts to win customer loyalty.

One of the most powerful tools in relationship marketing is giving something of value unexpectedly to your customers, some benefit they weren't anticipating when they chose to do business with you. It is a very effective technique in minimizing resistance to "being sold." A good example of how this technique can be used is the manner in which radio stations give cash or merchandise to random callers. The opportunity to win something of value creates listener loyalty within a significant segment of the listening audience.

Here are a few more examples of the creative use of this technique:

Suppose you own a beauty salon. You believe that the best way to increase volume is to offer significant discounts to attract new customers. But you don't want to cannibalize business from your existing full-price customers, or alienate them, and you don't want to cut prices across the board. What, other than cutting prices, can you do? Put on your thinking cap. You could invite customers to a free seminar at your salon on "the miracles of plastic surgery," booking a local plastic surgeon as your guest speaker. You'll be able to attract new clientele, have an opportunity to talk to your present customers, and hopefully bring back inactive patrons - and the doctor may get a new patient or two. In a similar vein, a Florida real estate agent offered home improvement classes to customers and prospects, presented by local contractors. He used his office as a class site. Prominent displays of his listings were placed throughout the office. During breaks in the presentations, attendees were able to preview his listings, and he was able to mingle and talk with them in a non-threatening environment.

Now you're a chiropractor. You're not getting the repeat business that you would like, and you've found that advertising is too inefficient and expensive. What else can you do? On goes the thinking cap. Go back to basics. Use the phone to call former patients. The telephone is still the most effective and fastest way to communicate with a client - faster than the mail, faster than a personal visit, even more effective than e-mail. Everyone picks up the phone and answers it, or at least checks messages. A phone call is personal and impressive - it demonstrates that you care about your patients' well-being and are willing to take the time for a follow-up call. Of course, the call has a dual purpose: first, to let your customers know you care about them, and second, to announce things such as new hours or services, or special offers. This technique lends itself especially well to voice broadcasting, because it is easily scalable - if you have a large customer base, it could take forever to call every one personally.

You just opened a carpet-cleaning company, and you missed this year's "Yellow Pages" listing deadline. You want to create awareness in your area that you are open for business, so you decide to personally visit retail carpet stores in your area. Offer them a special cleaning program that they can give to customers who purchase new carpet, and explain how that can help them sell more carpet. You will obtain new customers, and the carpet store sells more carpet. A win-win situation!

You operate an auto repair shop. In this type of business, customers don't come in unless they have a problem. You decide that an approach to generating goodwill would be to notify your customers that you will give them a free diagnostic and safety inspection during slow periods at your shop. You'll surely discover that some cars need repair work, and this could more than offset the cost of the inspections.

You own a local pizza joint. Your competition consists of large national franchise stores, and even though you offer competitive pricing, free delivery and frequent-buyer discounts, they still have the edge on you because of their name recognition. So, what else can you do? Offer your customers an unexpected bonus with each pizza, such as a free soft drink or house salad. This sets your business apart from the franchises, which will continue to do business as usual. Additionally, start a simple database listing each customer's preferences, such as their favorite toppings (this doesn't have to be high-tech. A simple 3x5 card will do the trick). The next time the customer calls to place an order, ask them if they want "the usual." It will surprise and flatter them that you remember them and what they like, and will go a long way toward building customer loyalty.

These are just a few of hundreds of possible examples to get you thinking about how reward programs can work in your business. Remember that reward programs must be legitimate offers of benefit to your customers, not sales come-ons, if they are to work.

"Money doesn't grow on trees...
It grows on databases."
- Jason Hartman

_∾ Chapter Six _∾

AutoMagic Marketing™

IN-TOUCH TECHNOLOGY –
A POWERFUL MARKETING TOOL

How much new business do you think you could generate if you could leave a personal message on the voice mail or answering machine of every prospective client? How much loyalty and allegiance would you build with your present clients if you could contact them with a compelling message that would be of benefit to them? Suppose you could have all the time you need to rehearse your message, perfecting it until you had just the right wording, inflection and enthusiasm? What if you could personally wish all your customers a happy birthday or anniversary without ever having to remember a single date? Your message may be business related, or something of a more personal nature. For example, your client may have mentioned that he likes jazz, and your message might simply inform him about upcoming local jam sessions.

Where will you find the time to do all this and still run your business? Welcome to the wonderful world of voice broadcasting. Voice broadcasting enables you to record a voice message and send it to a predetermined database of your clients' phone numbers automatically. The system only seeks out answering machines and voice mails. When it finds one, it leaves your voice message. If instead of an answering machine, a person answers the telephone, you are able to either leave an alternative voice message, or hang up to terminate the call. However, it's rude to just hang up, and it irritates the person answering the phone, so I suggest you opt for a polite message explaining the purpose of the call, and why you use computerized messages. Remember, this is all about relationship marketing, and you should never lose sight of the fact that good relationships and abiding by the Golden Rule are your central focus. It's not only about sales!

Being able to leave your message on the answering machines and voice mails of your clients enables you to keep in touch with them as often as you like (if your business is small and you don't have a large customer database, voice broadcasting can also be a powerful prospecting tool).

Of course, technology can be a boon or a bane. While many companies effectively use technology to generate leads and manage their databases, few actually timely and adequately follow up, and the leads that are generated are often lost. If used properly and judiciously, voice broadcast technology can foster relationships by adding a personal touch to your business, and it expands your ability to nurture your relationships with a broad spectrum of prospects and existing and former customers, without personally having to make time-consuming one-at-a-time calls. The system works like this: you periodically download new leads from a system called interactive voice response, via the World Wide Web, into your voice broadcasting system. Then you cue your prepared message to these new leads or customers and in seconds, each one receives your pre-recorded message via a phone call. Voice broadcasting is capable of handling thousands of calls per hour.

In today's world, most businesses face intense competition, and it is growing more intense every year. As larger and better-funded companies squeeze small companies, the future of small business ownership might look rather bleak. Technology can be the great equalizer, and the small independent business owner can help level the playing field by creating powerful technology-based systems, and then focus on running the systems, thereby leveraging limited resources.

In my business (residential real estate existing home sales), approximately 20% of the agents are responsible for 80% of the transactions. Statistically speaking, the numbers are similar in other sales-oriented industries. This may be so because top producers work hard to maintain a competitive edge. They maximize the efficiency of their businesses by focusing on the productivity-oriented tasks of their businesses, such as meeting with their clients to close sales and using technology-based systems wherever possible to handle activity-oriented chores such as prospecting.

These top producers are also always looking for ways to improve client relations and communicate with them more often. Remember to "customize" your message to your clients so that it is unique and tailored to their particular needs. The result of such planning and execution, if it is done right, is that clients will call you, rather than the other way around.

A word of caution is in order here. Many people are not particularly impressed or pleased with "salesmen" calls. While you may think your message is the most exciting thing since sliced bread, many recipients will just consider your calls a nuisance. Since interactive voice response is a 24-hour system, the opportunities for abuse abound. Always put yourself in your customer's shoes and imagine how you would react to your own message. Sensitivity to your clients is one of the key aspects of successfully developing relationships with them. Always give them the opportunity to request that their names be deleted from your voice broadcast list so that you don't permanently alienate them. There are other ways to contact customers who object to your messages that are gentler and less intrusive than the computerized phone call.

REMEMBER, TRADITIONAL DIRECT MAIL GENERALLY ONLY RESULTS IN 1% TO 3% RESPONSE RATES. Direct mail is one of those ways, although only a small percentage of direct-mail pieces will ever be read. In most cases, the exposure you get is five seconds or less before the client discards your piece. But you can improve the chances of your prospects responding if you give them something, such as free merchandise, or free information oriented to their particular interests. To increase the effectiveness of your direct mail program, you can personally call each of your clients via voice broadcasting before you send your piece, and leave them a message to be on the lookout for important information about their special interest. The automated message that the customer hears is approximately twenty-five seconds long, more than five times the exposure of the average direct mail piece. Just be sure you don't squander the opportunity and disappoint them with a worthless ad!

While telemarketing can be effective, very few salespeople like doing it, and the prospect's perception is that telemarketers are annoying and unprofessional. Voice broadcasting is intended to harness the effectiveness of telemarketing, but minimize customer resistance. Voice broadcasting is able to contact a greater percentage of your database than a telemarketer could, and your entire message is more likely to be heard. Also, because the message is recorded, there is no variation, and you can convey exactly what you wish to convey each and every time, and you can maintain such qualities as voice inflection and tonality on each and every call.

By downloading leads from an interactive voice response system, and loading them directly into your voice broadcasting system, you'll ensure timely follow-up for all leads. You'll be able

WARNING:

Don't put your home on the market until you've read this!

Special Free Report –

How to Avoid 10 Critical Mistakes That Could Cost You Thousands of Dollars!

Selling your home can be a very stressful experience. That's why it's so important to prepare yourself as completely as possible. *Be informed – not taken!*

Educate yourself concerning your real estate market, how to get the most money for your home and the necessary steps to conclude the sale. These things can all be quite stressful for the inexperienced home seller.

Lack of preparation could cost you thousands of dollars. Don't let it happen to you...

Call NOW for your FREE Report
1-800-XXX-XXXX
Ext. XXXX
anytime 24 hours-a-day

This is a no obligation community service

Examples of direct response ads used at our real estate office.

(Special FREE Report! By Jason Hartman)

How to Buy Your First Home... and Appear Experienced!

Buying your first home can be intimidating. It's easy to be "rushed" into errors in judgement. The worst part is these errors could cost you for many years to come.

Avoid the 10 most common...frustrating...painful mistakes of first time home buyers! Following the ideas in this report will see to it that you make the best decision possible.

Stop Paying Rent Forever and Own a Home of Your Own!

Call anytime 24 hours-a-day
1-800-XXX-XXXX
Ext. XXXX for your FREE Copy!
Get started today...soon you'll be living in the perfect home that's just right for you!

This is a no obligation community service

Examples of direct response ads used at our real estate office.

to send a message to every lead within minutes and you'll be able to make initial contact with the prospect while their interest is still fresh.

Voice broadcasting systems are not expensive when compared to hiring a telemarketing staff, or using traditional advertising methods. There is an activation fee, a flat service fee, and a per-minute fee for calls. High-volume discounts are available, often dropping the cost-per-minute charges by up to 40%.

You needn't be concerned with the technology itself, just know how to use it. A secure server automatically loads your database files in minutes. You control the loading, managing and naming of customer lists. The system sends a confirmation message to you via e-mail when your list is loaded and ready to be broadcast. You can program the day and date of the start time and the day and date of the termination time for each list to avoid sending broadcasts during hours when live answers are likely (remember, since a computer can not carry on a conversation, the preferred outcome of each call is an answering device, not a live person). You can configure and send up to ten broadcasts at one time. You can also obtain a real-time call report detailing the number of successful messages left and failures (due to live answers, no answering machine, busy signals, or disconnected or bad numbers), with documentation for follow-up and updating of your databases.

For further information on voice broadcasting and interactive voice response, refer to Appendix 2 in the back of this book. It's worth your effort to learn how to use this powerful tool, which is designed to reduce or eliminate expensive telemarketing, and increase the efficiency of telephone usage in your business.

Be sure to comply with FCC and other rules and regulations regarding telemarketing, and be sure to keep and use a "do not call list." Refer to www.fcc.gov for more information on this important topic.

YOUR COMPUTER IS YOUR BEST WORKER

While close attention to the quality of your product or service is vital to the health of your business, and supervising and managing your salespeople and processes is certainly important, the process by which all of this takes place is equally worthy of your attention. Understanding and utilizing the capabilities of computer technology is no longer an option for a business owner or manager. It is a necessity! If you are unfamiliar with the newest systems and software, you owe it yourself to learn about them (and implement them) ASAP! Your computer allows you to store, sort, update and maintain extensive databases, but if you are using it only for that purpose, the technology is being largely wasted. It's like driving a Ferrari in rush-hour traffic. You are utilizing only a tiny fragment of its capabilities. Faxes, e-mail, and audio and video can now be quickly and easily downloaded and transferred from one computer to another. Application service providers (ASP's) offer another powerful tool, allowing you to do things previously only available to the largest firms.

COMPUTERS ARE A FACT OF LIFE FOR BUSINESS OWNERS TODAY.

Completing a sale is indeed a process, not an isolated event. Customer relationship management (CRM) has become a much more important part of overall business planning than ever before, and software programs, as well as ASP's on the Internet, are readily available to simplify this increasingly complex job (it would be helpful for you to visit websites such as www.salesforce.com and www.siebel.com for examples of this powerful technology).

As in real estate, where location, location, and location are the three most important aspects of a property's value, follow-up, follow-up, and follow-up are the three most important aspects of selling. According to an extensive seventeen-year marketing study published recently by *New Equipment Digest* magazine, 63% of the prospects that requested product information did not make a purchase until more than three months after their initial inquiry. Nearly 20% took in excess of a year to make a buying decision.

When asked about future plans, 87% of the people who requested information on a product or service expected to eventually make a purchase. Only 37%, however, actually made the purchase in fewer than three months. Without diligent follow-up, most of these prospects will likely be lost.

The Dartnell Corporation, a sales training developer based in Chicago, completed an even more revealing marketing study covering a broad spectrum of industries. This study, and a similar study by McGraw Hill's sales research department, found that eight out of ten sales are made after five or more contacts with a salesperson. This study also found that 48% of salespeople give up after the first contact, and 25% more give up on a prospect after the third call. In other words, 90% of the salespeople have quit trying before 80% of the sales would have been made! It's like running a marathon and quitting with the finish line in sight. Regular communication builds awareness until your prospect is ready to buy. It may seem ironic, but if you want to succeed more often, increase your failure rate!

Even though most salespeople know that statistical research indicates that most sales are made after the fifth contact with the prospect, follow-through is typically so deficient that most of their efforts are simply wasted. To build a successful sales process then, a company needs to ensure that at least five sales calls are being made for every viable prospect. If the results of most statistical studies agree that the percentage of closed sales increases with the number of contacts made, then it follows that the same would be true for future sales after the initial sale. The selling process does not end when a sale is made. Follow up!

As you can well imagine, all of this activity can generate a monumental scheduling headache, and can tax the salesperson's nerves. Here is where computers and customer management software comes to the rescue.

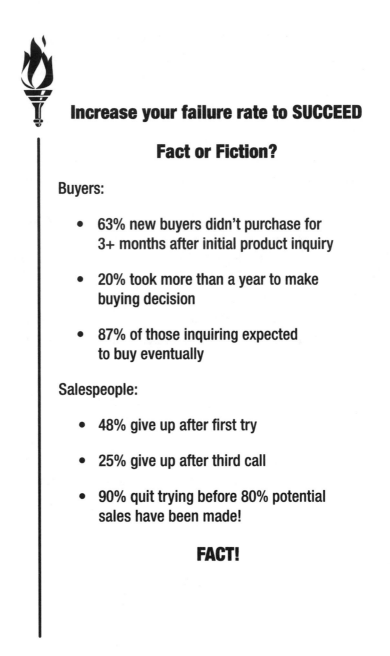

Increase your failure rate to SUCCEED

Fact or Fiction?

Buyers:

- 63% new buyers didn't purchase for 3+ months after initial product inquiry

- 20% took more than a year to make buying decision

- 87% of those inquiring expected to buy eventually

Salespeople:

- 48% give up after first try

- 25% give up after third call

- 90% quit trying before 80% potential sales have been made!

FACT!

MULTIPLY YOURSELF THROUGH AUTOMATION

The information in your client / prospect database provides you with the raw materials needed to create personalized marketing programs which can then be tailored to each individual client or, in the alternative, to a client segment.

As I've indicated, the full significance of what automated marketing can accomplish is not well understood by most small business owners who still use the computer primarily as a word processor or accounting device, merely producing invoices and reports, keeping track of accounts receivable, and handling correspondence.

A recent study done by the Academy of Producer Insurance Studies revealed the way many smaller firms view their computer systems. In the survey, 94% of the respondents considered themselves to be "automated" simply because they used some sort of computer system. However, when the same respondents were asked if they maintained customer information other than name, address, phone number and basic insurance policy information, less than one in four admitted that they did, and many questioned why they should bother to keep any other information. The quality of long-term relationships with their customers must surely suffer when the company knows only an account number, name, address and phone number. Yet, most companies keep and use little more than that basic information in their files.

Every modern computer system has some capacity for running automated marketing programs, but you should consider the following to optimize system performance:

- Is the data storage capacity of your system enough to meet your present and future needs?
- Can the information in your database be accessed and merged easily and quickly into customer communications such as letters and e-mails?

- What specific marketing functions are available?
- Can sales follow-up be automated so salespeople can focus on those prospects that are most likely to buy?

Some of the most useful sales information that you should collect is: 1) how recently has the customer purchased from the company, 2) how frequently has the customer purchased from the company, and 3) how much of the product or service has been purchased? The ultimate success of your program depends on the quality and quantity of your information and how often it is updated. You may wish to hire a data entry clerk to handle this task, but if the sales department has the resources, it is better for them to input their own data. No one knows the customer better than the sales representative, and no one should be privy to updated information. It should be a daily task for everyone to enter their own new data and update their own client information.

Create a profile for each customer. Remember, in relationship marketing, it isn't a question of what you want to sell as much as what your customers want to buy. Do adequate research to find out what your customers really want, and then make sure that is what you are selling. As you probe deeper, you will find that those in your targeted client group have many things in common. When you hear the same answers over and over again, you can assume that you are identifying basic wants and needs. Also, find out when they made their last purchase and what they purchased. How long have they been customers? As you conduct your interviews and gather information, watch for trends and common denominators. The process will take time, but it is well worth it.

The extent to which most companies interact with their customers is often little more than filling an order and sending out a bill. These companies engage in no further communication, unless the customer has a problem. Unfortunately, by the time the customer complains about a problem, it is often too late; more likely than not, that customer has been alienated and has already decided to take his future business elsewhere.

Create effective direct marketing pieces such as postcards, e-mails, display ads, brochures, newsletters, and proposals. The key to success in an automated marketing plan is to create promotional pieces that have the same type of impact as if you were sitting in front of your customers and talking to them face-to-face. Your marketing pieces allow you to be in front of a large number of prospects, as if they were one prospect at a time.

How many people responded to your ad? How many sales did you make as a result of your promotion? The marketing materials that you have, or that you create, are akin to "salespeople in print." They are a critical link in your sales chain. You wouldn't recommend that your salespeople take no more than five minutes to make a presentation to a prospective client, would you? Neither should your promotional materials take only five minutes to create. Tell your prospects the whole story, and fully explain the benefits of your product or service. In general, it is most effective to focus on one primary benefit to avoid confusing or overloading the prospect. Your marketing materials can also serve as direct response pieces and personal brand builders. Remember that through your materials, you are gaining access to your prospects' homes, so take advantage of the opportunity to promote yourself, as well as your products and services.

Develop a step-by-step system that will put your marketing materials in front of your customer or prospect at least seven times in a period of eighteen months. We've already seen that most sales aren't made until at least the fifth sales call, and your automated marketing program simply cannot be allowed to fall into the same category as the salesperson that quits after one or two sales calls.

GETTING YOUR MATERIALS OUT MORE THAN FIVE TIMES IS CRITICAL!

Applying these principles in a well-defined program will avoid the waste and frustration of giving up the sales effort prematurely. Instead of abandoning prospects that you have worked so hard to cultivate, follow through and you'll convert a significant number of them into customers. Always use your computer to help you stay in touch with your customers - by making customer contact automatic, you will more likely be there when they are ready to place an order.

It's advisable to routinely track the results of your various marketing efforts. Perhaps your newsletter isn't working as well as your e-mail alerts. You may be wasting too much effort and money on a full-color newsletter that isn't getting results. Or perhaps the quality of your newsletter isn't up to par and should be re-designed to higher standards. While a newsletter must be interesting and informative to succeed, it is still essentially an advertisement, and it should have all the elements of a good ad: an attention-getting headline and concise body copy that offers your unique selling proposition, and clear instructions on how and when to contact you for more information, or to place an order.

Make sure that your staff doesn't abdicate their responsibility to monitor the effectiveness of your advertising campaign. There is too much at stake to just leave it to chance. Salespeople are notoriously lax about paperwork. Hold them accountable for collecting feedback, keeping your database updated, and your automated system working properly.

In the final analysis, the best way to find out what's working and what isn't working is quite simple: ask your customers. Be honest and forthright. Ask them if they reacted positively or negatively to your automated messages. Let them know you're trying to design a program that is valuable to them and effective, without their being annoyed by it. Most customers are flattered that you value their input, and are sensitive to the effects that your sales efforts have on them. They will be happy to assist you, and your relationship with them can only be strengthened in the process.

By testing one sales technique against another, one price against another, one ad idea against another, one follow-up approach against another, you will eventually find the most effective, and therefore, the most profitable way to sell your products and services. Testing can be a simple and inexpensive process (or an involved and expensive one), but in any case, testing is vital to the success of your automated marketing program. Here are some testing tips:

Code every marketing piece, letter or ad that you send out. Codes can consist of a request to call a particular person or telephone number, mail to a coded address, or respond to a special offer or sale price. Document the results as returns come in. Make sure to instruct whoever handles your incoming calls to ask every prospect where and how they heard about the offer. Tracking isn't difficult. It just takes attention to detail and training your staff to actually do it.

Keep track of how much every automated marketing piece costs you to produce and deliver to your customers. Attach each current ad or letter to an analysis sheet. On the sheet, record the costs to produce and deliver the message as well as daily responses, and make cost/response comparisons on a monthly basis. Be sure to record the dates that the document was distributed.

Identify and refine the components of the documents that work the best, based on the data you've accumulated. Incorporate successful design elements into all new promotional materials, and modify current materials accordingly. Eliminate those elements that didn't work well, but don't automatically assume they don't work and discard them. You'll find that certain marketing pieces work better than others at different times of the month or year, or for different types of promotions.

When you identify that which works best, integrate those elements into your automated marketing system. The "winners" become the standard against which you test new ideas. As long as the standard control procedures work, keep using them, and continue to use them until you have tested something that works better. Keep in mind, however, that one of the most important things is change, to keep your promotions fresh, so that your audience doesn't grow bored with them, ignore them, or be annoyed by them.

Automated marketing not only helps you build sales success by allowing you to increase the number of qualified prospects that you can meet "face to face," but it also provides new ways of increasing sales and customer loyalty by cross-selling and up-selling related products and services (this has the effect of turning one customer into two or more). In today's highly competitive marketing environment, automated systems allow you to compete effectively with large franchises, chain stores, or better-capitalized companies. Without the scalability and cost effectiveness of these systems, you would otherwise be hard-pressed to reach enough prospects to grow your business sufficiently.

Now let's take a quick look at a few things you *shouldn't* be doing in your marketing program

TEN BIG MARKETING BOO-BOOS

Marketing Mistake #1

Designing institutional advertising or brand-building promotions without incorporating a direct response "hook." We've already established that having an aggressive and focused relationship-marketing effort in place with your current customers is essential. Even so, there is still a need to attract new customers.

Most advertising that you see and hear in the mainstream media is institutional advertising. Even at its very best, institutional advertising produces indeterminate and often deferred results. At its worst, institutional advertising is a waste of money and effort. By comparison, direct-response advertising, as its name implies, directs the prospect to respond by giving all the information that he or she needs to make a buying decision, and then gives instructions on how to place an order. Direct-response advertising can utilize both print and broadcast media. Just as in a face-to-face sales presentation, it makes a complete case for the company and the product. It is designed to overcome objections, offers all necessary information, and then asks the prospect to buy with a money-back guarantee.

Marketing Mistake #2

Not testing. I find it very surprising that so many companies do not test their marketing programs. They bet their futures on arbitrary, subjective decisions and on conjecture. The marketing function is often treated like a lottery, where dollars are thrown at a variety of approaches, hoping that something works.

First, marketing executives rarely have the inherent ability to know exactly what the marketplace wants. They have a tendency to shove products or services at consumers without first determining whether or not they really need or want what they are being offered. Relationship marketing, by its very nature, inquires and communicates with customers to find out what they want, and tailors products and services to meet those needs.

By testing one approach against another and getting feedback from customers, you can develop a well-oiled marketing machine that yields extraordinary payoffs. Settle for nothing less than maximum performance out of every marketing effort. Test, re-test and evaluate the results!

Marketing mistake #3

There is no unique selling proposition or clear delivery. Relationship marketing requires a tailored selling proposition (the "message") and effective delivery. Your unique selling proposition is the distinguishing advantage you hold in all of your marketing, advertising and sales efforts. It is the philosophical foundation of your business. It is what makes you stand out from the faceless crowd. Failure to develop a unique selling proposition for use in all of your marketing efforts will make your program almost as ineffective as the exclusive use of institutional advertising.

Your selling proposition is what makes your company, product, or service different from all the others. The formulation of your particular selling proposition depends on the specific market niche you have carved out or plan to attract. Whether your unique selling proposition is based on price, convenience, quality, selection, or some other aspect, it should pervade every public and personal message you disseminate about your company. It should become part of your brand identity.

Marketing mistake #4

No back-end effort. Most companies focus so intently on getting new customers that they forget to service and re-sell the ones they already have. Some companies pay lip service to their current database of customers, but few really mine the gold that this rich lode of customers offers them.

Marketing guru Jay Abraham uses a graphic case study in his seminars. He recounts how he helped a coin dealer structure an offer to sell an inexpensive starter coin set to attract new customers. The offer actually lost the dealer a few dollars on every sale. But of the 50,000 people who bought the promotional offer, nearly 10,000 eventually purchased an additional $1,000 or more of coins on the "back-end"! The dealer generated two million dollars of back-end sales! But that was only the first step. Every three months thereafter, the dealer sent another special offer to the 50,000 collectors who originally bought the promotional coins, and an average of 250 of them spent an additional $1,000 or more as a result of each offering. To further mine the gold that lay within his customer database, Jay showed the dealer how to go back for additional sales to his 10,000 repeat customers. About 1,500 of them purchased an average of $5,000 worth of coins within the next nine months! (There is another lesson in this story: collectors of things, whether they are coins, cars or Beanie Babies, can become obsessed with their hobbies. They tend to spend a disproportionate amount of money on their obsessions. If you can make your product "collectible," as Ty Toys Inc. recently did with their little "Beanie Babies" beanbag stuffed animals, you will have customer loyalty that will make your head spin - for a while, at least, until the fad runs its course!)

Repeat back-end sales are vital to any business. Without exception, every business needs a relationship-marketing plan to develop customer loyalty, along with a direct-marketing plan to generate new customers.

Marketing Mistake #5

Failing to determine the customer's needs. Most companies do little, if any, in-depth follow-up. They conduct no studies, no polling, no "farming" by geography, age, sex, nationality, income, family structure or employment. The companies that do focus on their customers' needs and wants end up with the lion's share of the business. The movie industry is a good example of how consumer tastes and preferences can dictate product design.

Marketing Mistake #6

Failing to maintain a high level of integrity and honesty in all of your business dealings. If you use too many tricks in your daily dealings with your customers, you may forget which rabbit you pulled out of your hat the last time you spoke to them. Success in business is often so simple and obvious that it escapes even the best magician among us - just tell your customers the truth. Treat them fairly and honestly, and be careful not to constantly try to "sell them something." A good example of the damage that can be done with gimmicky, heavy-handed sales techniques can be found in retail automobile sales. Salespeople in the auto industry are well known for haggling with their customers and using a high-pressure approach. No one likes to play the haggling game, and they don't like being high-pressured. Because of high-pressure sales techniques, auto salespeople get bad word of mouth, then have to make up for resulting customer resistance through price reductions and advertising. The high-pressure approach can be expensive! Why not replace this universally disliked practice with simple, straightforward, down-to-earth honesty? Saturn tried it - and it worked! Honesty and straight-forwardness are the strongest relationship-marketing tools you can use. Conversely, you can quickly damage or destroy the relationship by creating a lack of trust through dishonesty, high pressure or double-dealing.

Marketing Mistake #7

Failure to keep your company appealing, desirable, and fun with which to do business. Most companies never place themselves in their customers' shoes. If they did, they wouldn't make doing business with them so difficult or tedious. Every aspect of your business should be designed with your customers in mind. Are you convenient and accessible, appealing and fun? Do your customers feel better after doing business with you? Have they had a positive experience? Answers to these questions must be "yes" if you are going to maintain any sort of competitive edge. If you are a one-store company, you have to outperform the multiple-store chains to survive. Even if you are part of a large company, you will have to stay appealing. You won't find McDonald's restaurants in inaccessible places, nor will you find grumpy, unfriendly servers, poorly prepared food, or dirty restrooms.

Remember,

1 You can't provide too much service.
2 You can't make ordering too easy.
3 You can't educate or inform enough.
4 You can't follow-up and follow through too much.

Marketing Mistake #8

Failing to make clear to your customers the "reasons why." Whenever you make an offer, run an ad, voice broadcast a message, make a presentation, or ask for a sale, always let your customers know why they should deal with your company. The more factual, believable, and plausible reasons you give a prospect for dealing with your business, the more likely it is that they will become a loyal and repeat customer.

Marketing Mistake #9

Not staying with marketing campaigns that work. Businesses and marketing people often get tired of their campaigns long before the marketplace does. It is much the same with a popular entertainer who changes his repertoire and introduces new material. The singer tires of the old song long before the audience tires of it, because the audience doesn't hear it night after night, as the singer does. As a matter of fact, the audience comes to the concert because they want to hear the old familiar songs that they've come to love. By eliminating that which made him popular, the singer risks losing his loyal fans. The same is true of marketing campaigns. If you've tested and done your homework, stay with what is working. The only response to your message that is relevant is the customers'. If they are responding positively, stay with what is working. Test, retest and evaluate constantly. When sales start to taper off, then it's time for a change.

Marketing Mistake #10

Failing to focus clearly on your intended customer base. How many times have you seen an ad in a newspaper, or on TV, and not had the slightest idea what it was about, or for whom the information was intended? Even popular ads that are entertaining, controversial or stylish often do not have the intended result: selling the product. Don't presume that just because you know what your message is, everyone else will also. Neither should you fall in love with a stylish ad that doesn't clearly convey your message. Test your material to be sure it has the intended effect or you will be wasting your money or confusing your audience.

THE WONDERFUL WORLD WIDE WEB

By now, you may have already designed and built an Internet web site. If you haven't, make it a priority. I am sure you are well aware that the Internet is revolutionizing the way the world does business (in spite of the spectacular failure of many dot.com's).

> If you haven't gotten your business, products and services on the Internet, stop everything and get it done!

You can get all the information you need on this subject from website designers (usually kids under the age of 14) and Internet e-commerce consultants, in a variety of specialized books, and on the Internet itself, but I want to make a few pertinent comments:

- As with any marketing effort, carefully evaluate your response once you are up and running. You'll hear terms like "hits" and "numbers of eyeballs" as a measure of website success, but "hits" on the Internet consist of everyone who visits your site, including customers, browsers, and those who have accidentally stumbled on your site while searching for something else. All "hits" are

*Stop everything and get your business, products
and services on the Internet!*

not "customers." Customers are "hits" that buy something, or take the affirmative step of contacting you prior to buying something. As a "bricks-and-mortar" analogy, consider your financial future if you operate a very attractive store in a busy shopping mall, and all day long, you have browsers walk through your store....but nobody ever buys anything. How "successful" are you, really? Be sure the navigation bar on your home page includes a "contact us" link, with e-mail capability, and answer your customers' inquiries or orders ASAP.

- Register your business with the most popular web search engines and use carefully chosen key words. Creating a web site by itself does little, if anything, for your business. People need to want to visit, and be able to find your site, for it to have any value at all. They do this by utilizing web browsers and search engines to find products and services that they are interested in. If you're listed, they have a chance of finding you; if you're not, you may as well be the proverbial needle in a haystack. You wouldn't operate your business with an unlisted phone number, or without a sign on your door, would you? Make sure whoever is building your site uses the main search engines (such as Yahoo! or Google) to give your business visibility and accessibility on the Internet. And don't forget to re-submit your site to the search engines periodically (every 3 or 4 months should do it) to avoid going stale.

- Use direct-response banner ads - but use them carefully and judiciously. Banner ads were very popular in the early, heady days of the "dot.com" boom, but have become increasingly expensive, and increasingly ineffective, as the bloom came off the rose and more and more web users simply found them annoying, and now largely ignore them. These ads generally do not result in high response rates, partly because when clicking on a banner ad, users are immediately taken away from the site, forcing them to backtrack to their point of origin. Many just never bother to return. However, well-designed direct-response banners do allow potential customers to learn about your company and its products without leaving the web page they are viewing. These banners can also allow customers to fill out purchase orders, participate in contests, and request more information. A new form of Internet advertising, so-called "pop-up ads," may also be worth considering, though these, too, are viewed as increasingly annoying and ineffective.

Let's face it - the Internet is going to be playing a larger and larger role in business as the technology and executives' familiarity improve. The world has effectively been re-sized because of the Internet, having become virtually smaller than ever before. With the click of a mouse, you can access business and personal web sites from any part of the world, and you can conduct business anywhere without ever leaving your computer.

WRITE A MILLION LETTERS TODAY

As I have already stated several times in this book, the key to successful selling through relationship marketing is to maintain meaningful communication with your customers on a regular and timely basis. When you do this, and keep your personal brand in mind, when your customers are ready to buy, they will think of you and come to you first.

Of course, personal contact with each of your customers would be ideal, but if your customer base is large, that would be unwieldy or impossible. Even if you could maintain personal contact with all of your customers, you need something worthwhile to communicate, something of obvious benefit to them. In many cases, persistent personal calls can have a negative effect on your relationship; if you don't have a real benefit to offer, you will simply become a pest, and the customer will not continue to listen to you or want to see you.

If you offer a product or service that lends itself to personal calls, the best advice is to stay in personal contact with your "hottest" customer group, your "A" group. This group is your bread and butter, those accounts that constitute the majority of your business. It may be ten, fifty, or a hundred or more, but these customers are the bedrock on which your business rests.

The remainder of your database represents your potential - what it is that your company could be, and therefore, communication with this group is also vital. However, since you only have twenty-four hours in a day, by necessity you will have to stay in touch with them in other ways than personal contact.

Automated communication is the obvious answer, and we have seen that it can take many forms - voice broadcasting, which I have already discussed; e-mail, which works well only if you have e-mail addresses; letters, newsletters, information sheets, contests (such as the way radio stations often promote themselves), and surveys.

TWENTY-THREE SUREFIRE LETTER IDEAS

Letters and e-mails are an excellent way to stay in touch with your extended customer database. Letters can be personalized and sent out with your computer's help in a timely, scheduled fashion. Here are a few ideas for letters that you can easily adapt for your own purposes:

1   **New customer - "introducing our products and services"**
Many of your customers might be unaware of the full scope of your company's products and services when they purchase a particular item from you. If you've handled the transaction well and gathered all the information needed to remain in contact, it is an easy matter to remind

your customers periodically of your other products and services, or any changes or additions to your product or service line. It is also a great time to thank them for buying from you, and to remind them of the benefits you, your products and/or services offer.

2   **Good customer - "thank you for your business"**
Saying "thank you" to your customers is one of the most basic and effective relationship-building things that you can do. A simple thank-you letter or card makes the customer feel appreciated, and is a thoughtful gesture that they probably didn't expect. You can go a step further and enclose a discount coupon to be applied to their next purchase, or a special offer, or send them a certificate for a free lunch at a local restaurant. This is a better use of a portion of your ad budget than investing it all in mass-media advertising.

3   **Best customer - "survey, or preview of a new product"**
Asking your customers for their opinions of a new product or service you are planning to offer is a compliment your customers will appreciate. You will be surprised at the large number who responds. Make sure the comment card is simple and easy to use, and that you enclose a stamped, self-addressed envelope. Getting feedback from your customers offers you the opportunity to take the pulse of the market, build your relationships, set yourself apart from your competition, and lets your customers know that you appreciate them, and are trying to please them. You could also ask your customers to preview and critique new products or services. Let them use it for a limited period of time. Once again, the feedback will be invaluable in your market testing efforts (and you'll also find many

153

of your customers later purchase the product they preview).

4   **A new customer - "welcome to our loyalty club"**
As I've already discussed, businesses often use a club or V.I.P. card to recognize and reward their best customers. This letter informs your customers that they have been selected for membership, and outlines the club's benefits. Enclose a membership card with the customer's name already imprinted on it (ready to be activated when they join) to encourage them to participate in the club.

5   **Past customer - "we miss you and/or your business"**
Many businesses just write off and ignore lost or past customers, and focus instead on gaining new ones. A better approach is to try to regain the lost accounts. A simple letter with a generous "come back" bonus offer is often a successful way to have past customers feel that you really care about them, notice that they have taken their business elsewhere, and value them. Let them know that you're concerned about their past experience with your firm, and ask them for the reasons why they don't buy from you anymore - if they don't respond, you have lost nothing; if they do respond, you may have regained their business. Identifying and evaluating the reasons why lost customers stopped doing business with you can be far more important to you than getting new customers. Why? You want to nip bad business practices in the bud, before they are perpetuated and do irreparable damage to your customer relations. Just a small reduction in the rate of customer attrition can result in a very large increase in overall profit.

6 **Current customer - "upgrades and companion products"**
Many businesses offer upgrades from time to time, such
as is common in the computer and software businesses.
If your business or product lends itself to periodic
upgrades, make sure to keep an accurate database of
purchasers (a great source of customer information is the
"guarantee card" that you include with each product you
sell). Keep buyers aware of upgrades as they become
available. Hardware updates and new accessories also
should be offered to those customers. Companion
products can also be promoted in this manner. For
example, if you have a patio furniture company and you've
sold someone an outdoor patio set, you might offer them
an umbrella or barbecue grill to go with it.

7 **Current customer - "happy birthday or anniversary
wishes"**
It is very flattering to a customer to be remembered and
acknowledged on his or her birthday or anniversary.
Sending your customers cards on those and other
important days of their lives is a friendly and non-
threatening way of letting them know you remember
them and that they are important to you. Including a little
gift in the form of a discount coupon or a free lunch at a
local café is an even better way of showing them that you
care! Don't make this event a sales pitch, however, or what
should be a warm and fuzzy gesture can be viewed instead
as a cold and calculating exploitation.

8 **Current customer - "time for service has arrived"**
Many customers neglect or forget recommended periodic
service on major purchases like automobiles or
appliances. A simple reminder can help boost your service

revenue, and if done properly, your customers will think of it as a considerate way that you are helping them maximize the use and value of their purchases. For example, a real estate agent could establish cooperative ventures with a variety of home service companies such as pest control, lawn care, pool maintenance, carpet cleaning, etc. Send periodic letters to your clients, advising them of quality companies in the area that you personally recommend, and include special offers. Your clients will appreciate your thoughtfulness, and the companies that you refer business to will reciprocate, or in some other way compensate you for your referrals. It can be a win-win situation for everyone!

9 **Current customer - "new version of an old product, or a replacement offer"**
Every product has a limited useful life before it wears out or becomes obsolete. By staying in touch with your customers, you can inform them of newer versions of the products that are now available as upgrades or replacements. These letters can generate much higher response rates than the 2-3% of typical direct-mail pieces.

10 **Current customer - "personal invitation to a sale"**
If you are having a sale, why not send your customers a personal invitation? Include a special incentive for them to attend, such as an additional 10%-off coupon, or a gift that they can pick up at the sale location. Even something as simple as refreshments, such as coffee and hors d'oeurves will bring people out. Your customers should be treated as VIP's, and they should be given the courtesy of advance notice of sales, and special offers.

11 Current customer - "invitation to an event, seminar, or workshop"

Bringing experts, or, if possible, celebrities such as sports figures, politicians, media personalities and entertainers, offers your customers a chance to meet someone special, and offers you a chance to communicate with them and introduce them to new products and services. By having these events periodically, you bring your customers back into your place of business, and make them feel special.

12 Prospective customer - "quote follow up"

You've given current or prospective customers a price quote, and now you're waiting to hear from them. Follow-up letters are often more effective than phone calls because the prospect will feel less threatened or pressured by a letter. If you've given the quote adequate time, and the prospect hasn't responded, you may wish to offer an additional incentive in your follow-up letter, making it clear how highly you value your customers' business. Be careful not to appear like you're begging for business, however, and don't lower your quote to the point that the sale is no longer profitable.

13 Prospective customer - "inquiry follow up"

Inquiries about your product or service should be given top priority. A timely response is important - while you procrastinate, a more aggressive competitor may take the business. An inquiry is an invitation - use it to give your prospect all the information he or she needs to make an intelligent and timely buying decision. After your brochure or information packet is sent, follow-up letters should be mailed, which can contain additional information, or perhaps testimonials from past customers.

14 Prospective customers - "thanks for the referral"
When you get referrals, make sure you have a letter ready to go out quickly to the people who referred the business to you, thanking them for their thoughtfulness. A small gift will always be appreciated, and it will encourage your customers to continue making referrals. In general, you may want to actively seek referrals by advising your past clientele that you will be happy to reward them if they send their friends and social contacts to you. This is very powerful advertising, and it will be money well spent.

15 Current customers - "your account is past due"
Most customers know when their bills are due, but for a variety of reasons, they may be late in paying. To protect your relationship but still get the message across that you want to be paid, send a carefully worded, non-threatening friendly reminder letter that the bill is past due. Second and third letters can be sent as more time passes after a due date. Uncollectible accounts receivable can put you out of business. Not only are your customers using your money interest-free for too long a period of time, but also you need the cash flow to pay short-term obligations such as payroll, taxes, rent, etc. It's a good practice to have a policy of charging a late fee, and/or interest, on balances not paid on time. While you may feel that it's important to avoid offending or harassing your customers, you are probably not interested in operating your business as a bank making interest-free loans, or as a private welfare agency. At some point, you will stop worrying about offending deadbeat customers, and just want to be paid,

as you won't want to do business with them in the future anyway.

16 Current customers - "special incentive for early or on-time payment"

Another type of letter that is appreciated by customers is an incentive for timely payment. This letter reinforces the notion that not only should they pay your bill on time, but that they can receive better terms, such as a discount for prompt or early payment (discounts for timely payment are often incorporated in the original sales terms, such as a 2% discount if paid within ten days).

17 Current customers - "apology letter"

You can blunt the negative consequences of a mistake or foul-up by simply admitting that you were wrong, offer to correct the problem, and ask for another chance to win your customer's confidence. The judicious use of humor (self-deprecating or not) can reduce any hostility your customer might feel toward you, but be careful not to minimize the significance of your error, or slight or ridicule your customer in any way. A sincere apology demonstrates that you care, and that you want your customer to be satisfied. Just as referrals are a great way to build your business, insensitive customer relations are a very effective way to ruin your business and any credibility you have built. If a simple apology is not enough to appease a disgruntled customer, the tried-and-true gift certificate for a free meal at a favorite restaurant, a discount coupon or some other gift should help. However, don't beg, plead or grovel. Some customers are lost, and at some point, it is best to just let them go.

18 New customer - "thank you for your first purchase from us"

I'm sure you've worked hard and spent considerable money and effort to get new customers. A simple thank-you note expressing your appreciation for the opportunity to serve them can go a long way in building a long-term relationship. The little gestures already discussed, such as discount coupons, free gifts, or movie tickets will also be very much appreciated.

19 New or existing customers - "general follow ups"

Remember the statistics about how many calls it takes to close a sale? Well, the same can be said about building customer loyalty. Follow-up letters may be sent after a purchase, an inquiry, a complaint, or a referral. Just be careful not to overdo it. Something done every-now-and-then is a pleasant surprise. The same thing used over and over again, or too frequently, can become a nuisance. Too much of a good thing can become a bad thing!

20 Current customers - "news and information"

Letters to your customers containing information that you know is of interest to them is a good way of building long-term relationships. Ask someone in your office to read the local newspapers during down time or slow periods and clip significant news stories that may be of interest to your clientele. This gives you an opportunity to provide very specialized communication and relationship building with key customers. Obviously, you can't do this for every customer because you don't want to transform your office into a clipping service. But, on occasion, this is a very thoughtful and useful gesture to cement the relationships between you and your clients.

21 **Current customers - "seasonal offers"**

Many businesses or products are seasonal. Timely information will be appreciated and welcomed, particularly if the season is short and you remind customers about it so that they don't forget it, or forget you, and thereby miss the window of opportunity. For example, if you are in the produce business and a particular fruit has a short growing season, advising your customers can both improve your relationships and increase sales.

22 **Current customers - "special holiday reminders"**

Holidays such as Christmas, Mother's Day, Easter, or Halloween may represent special sales opportunities for your business. Informing your customers ahead of time about special holiday offers puts the thought of shopping at your store, or purchasing your products, in their minds.

23 **Prospective customer - "follow up a personal visit"**

A short letter thanking the prospect for their time after you have made a sales call or personal visit will set you apart from your competition, who may also have called on the client. Your letter will also remind your customers of your call and by the repetition afforded by the letter, effectively extends your presentation or conversation.

Your Brand Multiplies Relationships

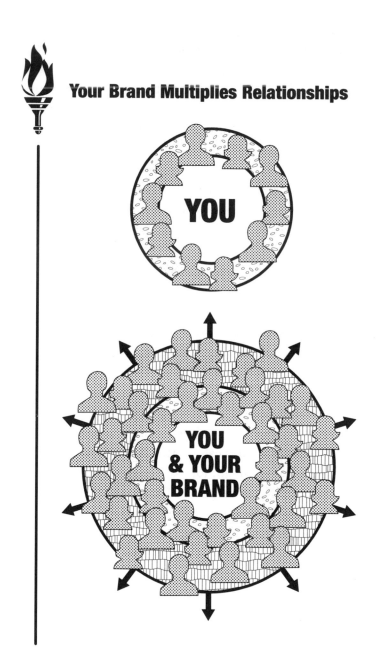

"Fashions fade - but style and character are eternal."
- Yves Saint Laurent

⟋ Chapter Seven ⟋

Become the Brand of Choice

JULIET WONDERED, in William Shakespeare's *Romeo and Juliet,* "What's in a name?" Unlike in Romeo's case, in business, your name can be the most important asset you have. Can you deny the value and importance of the name "Coca-Cola" to the company that owns it? Conventional marketing wisdom holds that a good name should be relevant, distinctive, memorable and flexible; however, a great name is a somewhat different story. A great name becomes the very essence of who your business and your product are in the eyes of the consumer. It goes beyond merely describing the features and benefits of your product. The brand name virtually becomes the product itself. How many times have you gone to a restaurant that sells Pepsi Cola and reflexively asked for a "Coke," or made a "Xerox" copy on another manufacturer's copy machine, or blew your nose into a tissue competitor's "Kleenex"?

Very few really great things come easily. Building an outstanding brand name takes considerable time and effort. It requires a long-term commitment, and every aspect of your marketing effort must be integrated with your brand in mind. Branding is a grand scheme strategy for corporate growth, profitability and stability, not just a way for consumers to differentiate between competing products and companies. I'm sure the Disney Company does not consider the name "Mickey" as just a way to distinguish their mouse from millions of other mice!

The benefits of building a successful brand name include the ability in many cases to command a premium price, generate greater sales volume, develop powerful customer loyalty, have more positive customer relationships, differentiate your product in ways that competitors can't easily copy, and have the ability to innovate rather than follow the lead of others.

Many marketing executives believe that the widespread accessibility of relatively low cost advanced technologies involved in the various aspects of a company's day-to-day operations have essentially leveled the playing field between large and small organizations, so that new ways must be found to maintain a competitive advantage. It is therefore more important than ever before to build a unique and powerful brand name, and use it creatively to establish market dominance. Once established, you must then protect the uniqueness and integrity of your brand vigorously. For example, anyone who has attempted to use Disney or McDonald's brands, copyrights, trademarks, logos, or characters without permission has discovered to their dismay (think "lawsuit") how protective such firms are of the brand identities they have created.

That being said, marketing executives often have difficulty building a successful brand. Careful attention and nurturing is necessary during the early stages of the development of your new brand. It's somewhat like growing an oak tree from an acorn. You bury the acorn in the ground and faithfully water it every day. But nothing seems to be happening as the seed germinates out of sight below the surface. You keep watering, and pulling out the weeds that threaten to stunt the growth of your invisible tree. You know

Consider all of the different things each of these symbols represent: type of product, quality of product, morality/ethics of the company, price range, etc.

that you need patience, diligence, and faith to ensure that the acorn sprouts and that the seedling is protected until it grows strong enough to survive on its own. Eventually, your acorn becomes an almost indestructible oak tree, which will survive many storms, as long as you do not allow it to die from neglect. Of course, there are rare instances of brands which just seem to catch on spontaneously, such as occurred with the Ty Company's recent "Beanie Baby" stuffed toys fad. However, that kind of success happens as often as winning the lottery, and should not divert attention from the reality of spending money and time to accomplish the objective the old-fashioned way - with hard work and patience.

An emphasis on branding requires the marketing executive to expand on many of the principles that he or she may have learned in business school. Modern marketing requires that product design be dictated by the customers' wants and needs wherever possible (an external orientation), whereas branding is essentially controlled from within the firm. For many years, corporations who had achieved dominant market positions felt they could rest on their laurels and simply design and offer their products and services, and customers would buy them, whether they really liked them or not. More enlightened and aggressive companies entered the market after carefully studying the customers' wants and needs, and designed their products and services accordingly. The big companies soon realized that they were losing their traditional foothold, and grudgingly came to the conclusion that they would have to change their approach to win the new battle in which they were involved. Many well-known and respected brand names disappeared, or have been terminally damaged, because the demands of the marketplace changed faster than the companies could, or were willing to, adapt to them - consider the recent demise of the Plymouth marque as a glaring modern-day example of auto industry brand mismanagement. Successful present-day marketers have apparently learned from past mistakes, and constantly take the pulse of the market before making major decisions. They are willing to make changes to keep their brands fresh and in tune with the times.

You've Got What It Takes

"Branding" and "marketing" are actually very different processes. When asked, "What is a brand?" most people would probably answer, "a familiar logo," or "a widely recognized product," or "the name of a well-known company," or something similar. But while "brand" includes all of these, it goes well beyond such simplistic physical conceptions to include a whole range of emotional responses on the part of the consumer. The brand represents a level of quality, consistency and trust that makes the buying decision far less uncertain and stressful, because the consumer believes that he knows what he is getting, and can rely on the brand to deliver the expected level of reliability, quality and performance. The more intangible and implied characteristics that the brand name carries with it, the stronger and more successful is its existence in the marketplace.

The Walt Disney Company's brands, for example, evoke many diverse reactions that in the aggregate comprise the "personality" of the company, which can go so far as to convey the company's business ethics to the public. The Disney brand is extended through the Disney characters (Donald Duck, Mickey Mouse, Goofy, etc.), the animated and live action movie productions, the theme parks, the retail stores, the clothing, toys and other retail items, etc. All of these together comprise the Disney brand, yet none of them separately represents the entire Disney "image." Disney has carefully nurtured a "family values" wholesomeness that it wants the public to associate with its brand, and it would never be expected to market indecent or violent products. When even minor deviations from this self-imposed high ethical standard occur, there is a disproportionate chorus of disapproval from the populace and the media. The brand is a pledge of consistency of value and values no matter where the brand is found, so parents can trust that their children will not be harmed, nor will they themselves be offended in a Disney-controlled environment.

Therefore, as this example illustrates, unlike sales and marketing, brand-related values cannot simply be expressed explicitly (you wouldn't expect an ad proclaiming "we are honest and decent" to be sufficient to create a belief among consumers that your company is indeed honest and decent). These values must develop gradually, over time, just as personal relationships that gradually grow to include trust and mutual understanding. The customer expects consistency and reliability from the brands he or she knows and trusts, and consistent quality and service only comes with time and careful attention to detail. This is why branding is so different from the rest of marketing, and why success is so much more difficult to achieve.

Using the Disney example, how many of its amusement parks have you attended that were substantially different from the others? How many of its animated features deviated from its basic wholesome "family values" reputation? How many of its toys were repulsive, violent, or disturbing for children? The answers, of course, are "none" (or "nearly none"). The Disney brand was developed by design, according to a pre-planned and carefully controlled marketing strategy. Its brand is the company's promise to its customers, and it uncompromisingly keeps its promise. Customers can trust the company to live up to its reputation.

It should come as no surprise to you that the ultimate objective of a good marketing plan should be to offer the customer what he or she really wants. Demand should be "pulled" by the customer, not "pushed" by the company. Successful marketing executives are always prepared to adapt to the changing tastes and attitudes of their customers, and they are willing to abandon any pre-conceived notions they may have as to what the customer wants, if it turns out the customer has changed his or her mind. "The customer is always right" is far more than a cliché to these executives. An excellent example can be found with companies that produce trendy clothing. They know quite well how fickle the market can be - what is in style this year, will be out of style next year. If they fail to anticipate these trend changes, they can quickly be out of business, or stuck with unsalable merchandise.

Brand specialists, on the other hand, have a different job, and must take a somewhat different approach in developing the characteristics and personality of their brands. In creating a new brand, the company must first define the brand's objective - what is the purpose of the brand? They then decide the "pillars" or foundation of the brand - all decisions are made based on these pillars (those physical characteristics that make the product distinguishable from its competition). They must also create the intangible aspects of the brand (such as a reputation for uncompromisingly high quality, or a high-class snobbishness). Finally, the brand's tangible aspects must be defined. The desired image must originate with the company, its marketing strategy, and the products themselves - not from the customer. The customer reacts to the brand's character, but doesn't create it.

In addition to designing the brand, the company must obtain frequent and accurate feedback so as to have a clear picture of how its customers are reacting to its efforts. If the desired image is not being successfully developed and nurtured, changes in the strategy must be made. If the brand image is developing along the lines contemplated by the company, then obviously do more of the same. Once the brand is established, consistency becomes critical. Keep in mind the "New Coke" fiasco of a few years ago. What was so wrong with the original Coca-Cola that the company felt it necessary to fiddle with the formula that had been so successful for so many years? Coke's loyal customers raised a hue and cry when their favorite soft drink tasted different (even if they just imagined that it tasted different). The new taste wasn't necessarily worse. Or better. But it was different. The promise of consistency that the Coca-Cola brand stood for had been compromised, and the company fortunately reacted quickly to the negative feedback by dropping "New" Coke and aggressively promoting the original "Classic" Coke to re-assert its brand's integrity.

Often, a brand is an extension of the personality of the company's founder, or of a charismatic or famous spokesperson. For example, Steve Jobs made Apple Computer what it is today, and Colonel Sanders is Kentucky Fried Chicken. Martha Stewart, the person, is inseparable from Martha Stewart, the business empire, and the list goes on and on. These bigger-than-life personalities created the image, and then required that everyone in the organization support it. There were no committee meetings, no policy discussions, no suggestion box - these people knew what they wanted, and never deviated in building a consistent brand identity. There is no effective substitute for that key ingredient: consistency. Ultimately, every aspect of your business must manifest this consistency.

Do not confuse your product with your brand. They are two very different things. Your product (or service) consists of its shape, color, design, the purpose for which it is intended, etc. But your brand goes beyond these physical characteristics. Describing your product is relatively easy, but a definition of your brand must include complex psychological and intangible factors rather than simple physical descriptions.

If someone were to ask you to define your own personal character, what would you answer? It is practically impossible to accurately and completely comply with such a request because it is something that others must decide for themselves. It is the same with the character of a brand.

As an example, consider the recent near-death experience of Apple Computer. When Steven Jobs and Steven Wozniak founded

Apple, they created a product (and corporate image) that was considered innovative and somewhat irreverent, and Apple became a cult classic. Apple became the choice of computer buyers who wanted to make a statement - that they were not just following the crowd. After Jobs left Apple, the products lost much of their innovative edge and started to look like the competition. Gradually, Apple's share of the market dwindled until it became a minor player, losing money along with customers. Apple flirted with oblivion, until Steve Jobs returned to work his old magic and breathe life back into the brand.

It was touch-and-go for a while, but Apple was able to resurrect itself by going back to its roots, and the original character of its brand. Once again, it developed and promoted cutting-edge, innovative products, and once again, it became a cult classic. The lesson to be learned is that once the brand's character is established, it must be perpetuated and protected or its future will be seriously jeopardized.

PATIENCE IS A VIRTUE

It's not realistic to expect your brand to evolve and develop a unique character overnight. Consistency and predictability take time to develop. Could you really be thought of as "consistent and predictable" if you've only been around for a few days, weeks, or months? The whole point of branding is to convey to your customers dependable expectations about how your product or service will perform today, tomorrow, and next week. What you want to do is imbue your brand with predictability, so your customer is not wracked with doubt each time he or she needs to make a buying decision.

Marketing and selling have a shorter time horizon in that the primary intent is to stimulate the consumer to action...to go out and buy the product without delay. Therefore, the urgency of routine marketing can actually hurt your brand's development by not giving it enough time to germinate and grow.

If you have done the branding of your company and product properly, you have created a uniqueness that your competition will not be able to easily overcome. They may be able to copy the outward physical appearance of your product, but they will not be able to duplicate its intangible values, because those values and characteristics are unique to you. If you are true to your brand, and are consistent in every thing you do and say, a competitor's efforts to weaken you will probably backfire. If you do not give them the ammunition, they will not be able to fire at you.

Remember the Japanese copies of high quality foreign products that came on the market after World War II? Many of them looked like the originals, and may actually have been of high quality (such as the copies of German Leica cameras produced by Canon), but they had the "Made in Japan" label on them, and many consumers shied away because of the perception that Japanese products were cheaply made and of low quality. It took many years of producing high quality, innovative products before consumers came to view Japanese goods with the respect afforded them today.

While the immediacy of marketing, and the time-consuming aspect of brand building, may seem at odds with each other, they can, and must, co-exist in your company. Neither should be sacrificed in favor of the other - you will find it difficult to meet the competition head-on without effective advertising and *Don't lose* promotion, and your advertising will fall on deaf ears if you do not *track of the* have a recognizable brand. Your marketing program and your *goal as you run* branding strategy are two inseparable aspects of your overriding *the race.* objective of selling your product or service profitably, so that your company can grow and prosper. After all, what is being in business (and this book) really about?

To build your brand, customers need to become familiar with your products. Therefore, you should do whatever you can to get your products into the hands of as many consumers as possible. Creating demand is often the most important aspect for successful long-term branding. Special promotions, such as events related to holidays, are a very good way to gain market exposure, generate sales and attract new customers. However, promotions will have to make sense to be effective. The more significant the event to which you are relating your promotion, the more effective it is likely to be. In general, you are better off "celebrating" holidays such as the Fourth of July or Thanksgiving than events such as a new store opening or a company anniversary. This maintains a higher credibility factor, and is less likely to cheapen or trivialize your brand. Customers will see through phony "sales" or tired excuses to lure them into your store. Also, be sure that your promotions fit your brand's image, and that they uphold the values your brand is supposed to represent (if you are trying to project a "classy" image, don't dress up as the Easter Bunny and hop around in front of your store). If you have an interesting concept, consumers will want to visit you.

Such promotions are generally short-term in nature and are designed to produce immediate results, i.e., product sales. Companies should not use such short-term techniques as a brand-building methodology because branding depends on permanency and consistency and does not develop well in a short-term fragmented context. When incorporated into a well-designed long-term strategy, methods such as automated marketing (AutoMagic™) and other relationship marketing programs, can be very effective branding techniques.

Since successful branding ultimately requires a significant degree of emotional involvement on the consumer's part, try to involve your customers whenever possible by using phrases or images that play to their most basic needs, such as health, wealth, love and acceptance. The idea is to connect your customers on an emotional gut level with your brand of beer, car, or cigarettes, so that they believe that using your product will bring them the happiness and fulfillment that may be lacking in their lives. If you can accomplish that, you will have gone a long way toward establishing brand identification and loyalty. For example, Phillip Morris' *Marlboro Man* had nothing to do with the characteristics of the Marlboro brand of cigarette itself, but the image that was projected of masculinity, freedom, and adventure sold millions of cigarettes to people longing for the lifestyle that the Marlboro Man personified. While the sensible side of smokers knows quite well that smoking cigarettes has nothing to do with being adventurous and free-spirited (on the contrary, it could cost them their health or their lives!), the branding effect of the Marlboro Man certainly worked, and it became something of an American icon.

Consider also the physical appearance of the Marlboro Man himself (it wouldn't have made much sense to stress the appearance of the product being sold, since all cigarettes look pretty much alike, and package design alone wouldn't have done the trick). Suppose the promotion had been identical, except that the Marlboro Man looked instead like the stereotype of a computer nerd, rather than a handsomely rugged free-range cowboy, do you think the branding campaign would have been as effective?

That being said, the relationship between consumers and your brand is not unlike relationships among individuals. While being attractive might get you more dates, it does not necessarily get you a spouse. A beautiful person with an obnoxious personality will likely be a lonely and unfulfilled individual. If Marlboro cigarettes were the very worst cigarettes on the market, the ad campaign alone would not have been enough to build long-term brand loyalty and success. The product needed to be good (though not necessarily the best) to succeed. You must pay attention to the whole enchilada!

So it is the personality and character of your brand, more than just eye-catching packaging and pizzazz, that is necessary for the development of a long lasting bond with the consumer. How do you let people know your character? Do you buy TV spots that say, "We're a great company and our products are the very best there are!" No, that is perceived as just another self-serving commercial. Character is earned through consistent behavior; it takes time, it is not told or sold. And it is fragile. One slipup can destroy years of hard work. Jack-in-the-Box restaurants (tainted food), Tylenol pain relievers (tampered product), Firestone tires (manufacturing defect), and ex-President Bill Clinton (lapse of personal integrity) can all attest to the high price that is paid for slipups (as these incidents demonstrated, however, strong brands can eventually overcome slipups with good damage control). Once your reputation is tarnished, or destroyed, you may never be able to repair it, or it may be salvaged only with the passage of time and significant financial expenditure. For these reasons, if you really need to change your brand's character, it must be done carefully and slowly over time, not abruptly. Coca-Cola learned that lesson the hard way, with the introduction of "New Coke." If the change is too abrupt, it can be perceived as an abandonment of the qualities that made the brand successful, and the new element of uncertainty that is introduced will cause customers to pause before making what was previously an automatic decision to buy. That can negate the reason for developing the brand in the first place - building customers' trust that the product will deliver consistent and reliable quality and performance.

Character sets the tone of all advertising efforts. Once established, the character of your brand is further enhanced and sustained by all of your advertising and promotion. Like the brand itself, your advertising must have continuity so as to impart an aura of reliability and trust. Very often, short-term disappointments in sales growth, or loss of market share or momentum, result in a company changing its advertising agency, or marketing manager. A change in the company's advertising philosophy itself often results. This can have the effect of changing the public's perception of the brand, possibly to its detriment. Similarly, the sale or merger of a company can take its promotional efforts onto a different track to conform to a new corporate culture. Such moves can also have damaging effects on the brand. If the latest marketing trends suggest that you do something other than what you have been doing, be very careful if you plan to deviate from your over-riding branding goals or corporate image.

If your goal is to build long-term relationships with your customers through relationship marketing and Personal Branding, then a carefully crafted and consistent program is a must!

"Things could be worse. Suppose your errors were counted and published every day, like those of a baseball player."
- Anonymous

⟨⟩ Chapter Eight ⟨⟩
The Media Is Your Ally

WHETHER IT'S COMMUNICATING with prospects or existing customers, the proper use of the mainstream media can be vital to your company's success. Unfortunately, too many companies allow the media to manage their advertising, and thus relinquish control of their communication with their customers to a frequently unqualified third party. While the media can surely be an important ally, it should not become the tail that wags the dog. It's too easy to rely on the media to do your job by default. Don't relinquish control over such an important function to people who have only a passing interest in your success!

When I speak of the mainstream media, I'm referring to print (such as paid-circulation newspapers and magazines, and free circulation publications), radio, television (cable and network), outdoor (billboards), direct mail (use of fliers or letters via the post office or hand-delivered, or joint-ventures with other companies), and Yellow Pages directories (a specialized form of print media).

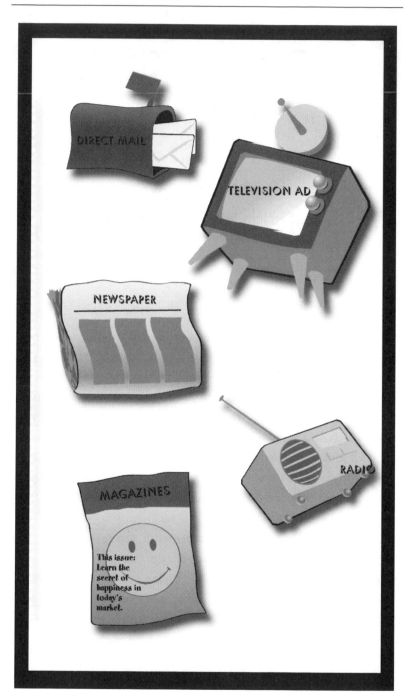

THE GOOD, THE BAD, AND THE UGLY

Let's consider some of the advantages and disadvantages of each of these media channels, and some creative ways to use them:

PAID CIRCULATION NEWSPAPERS AND MAGAZINES

Advantages

Paid circulation means that the reader requested that the publication be sent to him or her, and paid for it. It is a virtual invitation into the reader's home. Ad response rates are often 5-6 times higher for paid subscriptions than for free, mass-mailed publications.

Disadvantages

Paid advertising in newspapers and magazines can be very expensive, depending upon the nature of the publication and its circulation. Print ads are often limited to black and white (color can triple the cost of an ad), they are not animated, and the reader can't interact with them. Publications are often rigid in their business policies and can be difficult to do business with.

Bargains available

Publications often run "special sections and editions," which are often targeted to particular groups of readers. Since these special promotions are for the benefit of the publication as well as for the advertisers and its readership, you may be able to negotiate a better ad rate. As with most things in life, ask and you may receive. Also, ask your ad sales rep if the paper/magazine offers what are called *stand-by ads*. These are ads that are pre-composed and often sell for half, or less, of the cost of a conventional ad. Also, don't overlook possible bargains that may be available in classified ads. It is a high readership section of the paper, and since it is "classified," or sorted by topic, there is an excellent chance that your ad will be read by people looking for what you have to offer. Three-and four-line classified ads often have more impact than display or boxed ads on another page of the paper, and they are almost always cheaper. More readership for less cost is an unbeatable combination!

Be aware of co-op opportunities. You may find manufacturers, industry associations, or wholesalers who will offer to pay a portion of your advertising costs if they can cooperate with you, or piggyback on your ad. There are usually restrictions and additional paperwork, but this arrangement could well be worth the extra work since it represents a partner who will share the costs.

Always be on the lookout for editorial opportunities, which can be gold mines for your business. Publicity is nearly always preferable to paid advertising because it has more credibility and usually costs little or nothing. A feature story can be a tremendous boost for your business. The trick is to get a reporter's attention and generate enough interest for him or her to write a story. You will have to be someone interesting, or do something that is newsworthy, and then be sure to effectively communicate that to the proper reporter(s) at your selected publication(s). Reporters and news writers are always on the lookout for stories by poring through news releases, following up leads, and scrutinizing other media for interesting story ideas. Here are some tips to help you stand out and get your story published:

Develop relationships with selected editors and/or reporters.
Provide your media contacts with worthwhile story ideas, whether they relate to your business or not. Reporters love to develop contacts with people who have a nose for news. You could

also write and submit your own features, letters to the editor and news bits.

Offer to share your expertise by writing a regular column, or as a periodic contributor to the publication. Often editors and reporters will start to seek your "expert opinion" when they are working on a story. Once you have established yourself as an expert in your industry, the media will come to you.

Write and submit stories about your clients or customers, including information about unusual interests or hobbies, lifestyles or significant newsworthy events in their lives (contact your clients and ask for their written permission before discussing anything about them publicly. Never risk embarrassing yourself or your client, or having a lawsuit filed against you by publishing or disseminating personal information without first getting permission, and checking the accuracy of your information). Try to "proof" your story before it is published - sometimes a reporter will misrepresent your business with incorrect titles, misspelled names, etc. If done properly, you will develop great relationships by helping your customers look good in the community. You can use the opportunity to plug yourself and/or your business in the article, but avoid blatant attempts at self-promotion. You can request that the reporter work in a promotion for your business if it's newsworthy, but don't insist on getting free advertising in what is ostensibly a news story. That's never appreciated in a newsroom, and it can turn the reporter off and ruin your budding relationship.

FREE PAPERS AND MAGAZINES

This includes *Pennysavers*, shoppers, niche publications, real estate listings, auto traders, and any other giveaway publication that derives its revenues from advertising alone. Look for those with widespread availability in your area, usually in places like super markets, convenience stores and sidewalk vending machines, as well as those that are mass-mailed.

Advantages

Free publications usually offer advertising space at a much lower cost than their paid-circulation counterparts, and often have loyal readers and wide circulation within their market areas. Pricing for advertising may be negotiable, so always try to get a better deal. Free publications also tend to be niche-oriented, appealing to readers with particular interests or similar demographics. If these happen to be your target customers, you may find the niche publication works very well for you.

Disadvantages

Circulation is often exaggerated. It is wise to ask for audited information. Most legitimate publications of this type will be able to provide audited distribution figures, although even those figures are questionable since so many of the copies are simply thrown on lawns, put in supermarket racks, mass mailed, or piled on store counters. You should be looking for large distribution figures, but more important, large readership numbers. Don't advertise in these publications just because the price is low - so might be the actual readership.

Bargains available

Free publications are often flexible on their ad rates. Negotiate, and ask about "on deadline" specials.

Other considerations

Many publications allow their regular advertisers to write articles, author periodic columns, or run paid news-style stories about themselves or their businesses. If this is the case, take advantage of the opportunity as often as possible, and take the time to write a good story - one that will have maximum impact. If writing is not your strong point, and you have the opportunity to get this type of exposure, hire a professional writer to compose the article or column for you.

Many free publications have a shelf life of a week or more. The longer your advertising is in the marketplace, the better the chance that people will see it. When your ad runs in a daily paper, its shelf life is one day; when it is placed in a monthly publication, the shelf life is thirty days.

Classified ads are often very effective in the "shoppers" and free publications. They are the most cost-effective way to reach the publication's audience. It's easy to get lost in the clutter, however, so be clever when writing your classifieds. Do your very best to make sure they get attention and have impact.

RADIO

Radio can be a very effective advertising medium since there is an average of 3.5 radios in every American household, and most people listen to the radio at some time during their day.

Advantages

Radio ads can be generated within an hour if necessary. If your message has urgency, radio offers the fastest way to get the word out via the mainstream media.

Radio stations target their programming to specific age groups and listener demographics. Pop, rock, jazz, country, talk radio, oldies, and classical all have their loyal listeners. By matching your targeted customer base with the radio stations most likely to reach that audience, and placing your ads accordingly, you can get worthwhile results.

Radio is still a relative media bargain. Ad spots can cost as little as a few dollars each, although peak commuter drive time, and other prime time slots, usually cost much more than ROS (run of station) times. Since the ad has little, if any, value if it falls on deaf ears (nobody listening), in radio, as in virtually everything else in life, you get what you pay for. It will usually be worth the extra money to advertise when the listener count is highest. With a large radio buy, you may be able to negotiate a station appearance for your business or more spots free of charge.

Disadvantages

To be effective, your ad needs to air over and over again. Your audience's radios have to be turned on, and they must be tuned to the station on which your ad is running, and they need to be listening and paying attention for your message to get results. Radio sales reps will recommend running your ad twenty, thirty, fifty times or more in a given time period (not a surprise, since they usually work on commission), turning any initial price advantage into a disadvantage.

Radio is also a very competitive medium, and listeners can be ruthlessly fickle. When a listener doesn't like a song, or an ad, or the disc jockey, a touch of the button is all it takes to listen to something else. Individual markets may have ten to twenty radio stations or more to choose from (digital satellite radio may also significantly change listening patterns, but it's too early to say for sure, as of the date of this writing). Also, it's not only the content of your own ad, but the quality and appeal of the rest of the station's programming which determines the effectiveness of your offering. Make sure you ask for Arbitron ratings for the stations with which you plan to advertise.

Bargains available

Radio ad rates are rarely fixed. You can generally negotiate prices, and the better you are at negotiating, the lower the rates you'll likely pay.

Here's another approach: radio talk shows, how-to shows and interview shows, are all excellent opportunities for you to position yourself as a local expert and make yourself a local celebrity. Not every radio station is open to this idea, but if you have interesting content, unusual style, or an engaging on-air personality, you'd be surprised what many stations will do to obtain your ad account. If you have a product to sell, send a sample to the morning DJ's and talk show hosts. Often, they'll talk about you on the air, especially if you have something unique or especially interesting to offer. However, there is some risk, since you can't control what they'll say.

Get involved in radio giveaways and contests. Everyone wants to win something, and radio is really good at this. It doesn't cost much, and you reap outsized rewards by involving a large segment of the station's listening audience.

TELEVISION

The average American home now has 2.5 television sets, and the average viewer spends approximately 4.5 hours per day watching (of course, more and more of this time is spent watching cable stations which may not have paid advertising slots). No other mainstream medium can claim such a following (the Internet is rapidly catching up in terms of contact hours, but Internet users are far less likely to spend 30-60 minutes at one website, and they are even less likely to watch commercials or read on-line ads). Not only do TV viewers respond to traditional commercials, but also they are becoming more and more willing to order merchandise from direct-response and infomercial-type promotions.

Advantages

Like radio, television offers advertisers a wide selection of time slots in which to air commercials. It can draw a huge audience during prime time.

While newspapers are strictly visual, and radio auditory, television has the advantage of being both, offering color, energy, movement, sight, sound and special effects. Furthermore, TV can be interactive, via the use of infomercials (from short commercial-length spots to the lengthy 30-minute variety). Customers are able to purchase the advertised product immediately through the use of an 800 number and their credit card. It may also be possible to tap news shows for exposure. Invite a local news personality to your business location for a live on-air show. If you're newsworthy and lucky, you may get 10-15 minutes of free exposure!

Disadvantages

Television was once a very affordable medium, but with the possible exception of local cable channels, that's no longer the case. Costs not only include airtime, but also all of the production costs associated with the commercial. Some cable TV companies will produce your ad for a fraction of the cost of an ad agency. Typically, the more innovative and interactive the spot is, the higher the cost. Network advertising is typically two or three times the price of cable television advertising.

"Channel surfing" via the remote control has become something of a national pastime in America. The wide variety of television programming that is available in most communities is usually two or three times higher than the number of radio stations. Some cable and satellite systems offer hundreds of stations from which to choose (while there may not be as many viewers for a particular station, cable programming does provide the opportunity to select a more targeted and better quality audience). However, as with radio, this all means nothing if your audience is not tuned in, and paying attention to your ad!

Television advertising has an inherent negative characteristic that is difficult to overcome: is your appreciation for a program sponsor and its products enhanced when you are engrossed in your favorite program, or an exciting movie, and a commercial interrupts at every critical juncture? I doubt it. Stations have tried many ways to overcome the tendency of viewers to run to the refrigerator or bathroom when the commercials come on, including increasing the volume of the ads, but many viewers mentally tune them out no matter what. Your best bet is to make your commercials more interesting than the show (not an insurmountable task considering the quality of most programming today!). You will need to create a compelling, entertaining 30-second "movie" if you expect to win the battle for the viewer's attention.

OUTDOOR ADVERTISING

Billboard advertising has come under heavy criticism in recent years from environmentalists, the "taste police," and others who feel that outdoor advertising is nothing but an eyesore. Some highway systems, especially heavily traveled interstates, have abolished billboard advertising completely because of fears that it distracts drivers, and many others severely limit its use. Still, billboards remain an unmistakable fixture along American highways and byways.

Advantages

Billboards generally remain in place for a month or more, and can be permanent fixtures on the skylines of many communities (in fact, many are actually painted on the sides of buildings). Advertisers, trying to set their billboards apart from the clutter, and attract attention, have become very creative in their designs.

Outdoor sales representatives use the term "impressions" to designate the number of cars that drive by an outdoor sign during a given time interval (usually a month). The numbers can be very large, particularly along heavily traveled highways leading in and out of major metropolitan areas. An unintended advantage to the advertiser of these busy routes is that many rush-hour motorists are slowed to a crawl, and there is your billboard, staring them straight in the face. Being a captive audience, with little else to do, they will read your message over and over again, whether they like it or not (they'll even have the time to jot down your contact information, such as a phone number or website).

Disadvantages

Outdoor signs can be expensive to produce and expensive to rent. Even with the "impressions" numbers being as high as they are, they are generally not very good for direct response type advertising because few drivers have a pen and paper handy to copy your contact information (even the ones stuck in rush hour traffic). However, they are exceptionally good as information and directional aides ("Eat at Joe's Diner at the next exit").

There is always the annoyance factor with which to contend. Just as commercials that interrupt favorite TV shows can be resented, outdoor signs can be viewed as eyesores that detract from the enjoyment of a pleasant drive. One of the basic rules of advertising is to avoid having your messages create a negative reaction in your audience. It is often said that being noticed is the only important thing, but I do not believe that for a minute. I can think of several controversial and offensively tasteless ad campaigns of the past few years that left a very bad impression, and I swore that I would never patronize those companies or buy their products!

By necessity, billboards can't say very much. As drivers whiz by, focused on the road ahead of them (except at rush hour), they usually have only a split second to notice your ad. If the billboard is too wordy, very few people will read it. A rule of thumb is to limit copy to seven words or less. Ideally, the ads should include eye-catching graphics, your name, and your phone number. But, as I have already said, how many people are driving with pen and paper in hand, ready to jot down phone numbers on billboards?

Bargains available

Very few, but never stop looking. While less heavily traveled locations are usually less expensive, you generally get what you pay for. If nobody sees your ad, it does you no good.

DIRECT MAIL

We've already discussed direct mail, but this is a good context to review some of its advantages and disadvantages. With all the negative talk, there must be some measurable advantages to its use - the post office delivers hundreds of millions of pieces of direct mail advertising every year. Why would there be so much of it if it didn't work?

Advantages

At the very least, mail delivery is a sure-fire way to get your message into peoples' homes. You can be sure that every recipient at least touches the item that you've mailed to him or her. Whether it is read or not is another matter, but at least the delivery method is effective.

Unlike print, where an ad is priced by the column inch, or radio and television, where price is based on the length of time the commercial runs, and how often it is aired, direct-mail pieces can be anything from an inexpensive postcard to a fat (and expensive) full-color catalog. Since you have to catch the recipient's eye and interest in the brief instant between receiving it in the mail and throwing it in the trashcan, it should have high initial eye appeal, be in vibrant color, and be as interesting and informative as you can possibly make it.

Disadvantages

Although it's guaranteed to be touched, however briefly, less than 40% of all direct-mail pieces are ever read, and the rest wind up in the nearest trashcan. The likelihood that someone will actually make a purchase as a result of a direct mail piece is estimated to be anywhere from 1% to 3%, at best, which means that only one to three in one hundred will actually make a purchase as a direct result of it. Thus, like most mass media advertising, there is a very high waste factor.

Some forms of print or other mass media advertising cost literally pennies per household. Direct mail, on a per-household basis, can cost many times that amount. As an example, suppose you plan to mail 10,000 full-color, 8-1/2 x 11 fliers. If it takes one person four hours to prepare the flier, then it may cost you $50 in labor. It may then cost $1000 to print the flier, at $0.10 each, and an additional $0.03 each for the mailing label, which requires six man-hours to attach at $10/hour, for an additional expense of $360. Mailing the fliers using a bulk mail permit costs $0.20 each, for a total of $2000. You have by now invested $3,410 in this rather limited campaign.

Suppose that you are offering a $75 carpet-cleaning special in the above example. Based on average statistical expectations, you can project a response rate of approximately 1%-3%, for total sales in the range of $7,500 - $22,500. Assuming profit margins are typically 20% for your business, you could have lost as much as $1,500 or realized a profit of up to $1,100 for all your effort. This is a good example of calculating the overall returns from such a direct mail campaign, and points out the importance of careful planning and cost analysis before making the investment of time and money. You should ask yourself, "Is there a better way to get results?" Carefully weigh the alternatives. Don't just do it and then keep your fingers crossed.

Bargains available

The postal service's rates are nonnegotiable, so you'll get no special deals there. But "marriage mail" (mailing your flier along with other companies' fliers) can reduce your costs considerably.

You might also want to consider other methods than the U.S. Mail to disseminate your message to save on delivery costs. Many merchants hire students to hand deliver flyers, or flyers may be inserted into home-delivered newspapers. Be creative.

YELLOW PAGES

For some types of businesses, the phone company's traditional Yellow Pages directories, and the new crop of Yellow Pages clones, and Yellow Pages online websites, seem to work well (see www.yellowonline.com and www.switchboard.com for good examples).

Advantages

The Yellow Pages have a long shelf life, as they stay in the customer's home or place of business for a year, and are automatically updated with new editions. Also, since they are sent to everyone with a phone, and are available on request by others, they get wide distribution within the local service area.

Depending upon the type of business you have, Yellow Pages can work well. If you are one of many commodity-type businesses, you can become lost in the crowd, however (have you checked the listings for "attorneys" or "auto repair shops" lately?). Design an eye-catching ad. You should also consider paying extra for a display ad rather than a basic listing.

Disadvantages

Yellow Pages ad rates have skyrocketed. For a three-line ad, the price can be about $300. For a display ad, the price can run $1,500 to $40,000 or higher. That's a large investment, and the ad will have to generate a significant amount of business to pay for itself.

Keep in mind that your ad is right next to every competitor you have. Yellow Pages advertising is the only mass medium that purposely places your ad in the midst of every competitor in the marketplace. How will you differentiate yourself so that you will be the chosen one (other than naming your business "Aardvark" to be listed first)?

Once printed, your Yellow Pages ad is unchangeable for a full year (proofread your ad carefully before it is published, since it cannot be modified until the next annual edition). It also shouldn't be used as a direct-response message unless you can guarantee that your prices (if included in the ad) or contact information (phone number, fax number, website or address) will not change during the year. While nothing prohibits you from using clip-out coupons in your ad, how many people are willing to cut up their Yellow Pages? Some Yellow Pages books offer a separate coupon or special offers section, however, and that may be worth your consideration if you believe Yellow Pages users look beyond the usually specific and limited purpose for their periodic use of the book, and will find your coupon offer. The point is, the Yellow Pages is not the type of book people pick up to thumb through, or look to for light reading.

Bargains available

Though limited, there are pricing bargains available in Yellow Pages ads. To get them, wait until the last day of the submission deadline, then negotiate the best deal you can. However, don't wait until the last minute to compose and design your ad. You may get a last-minute deal on the rate, but you don't want your ad to be any less effective than if you had taken a month to plan and design it.

OTHER MEDIA

There are a number of new technologies which have increased the choices advertisers have at their disposal to disseminate their messages, such as fax broadcast (whereby text and simple graphics can be faxed to a database of fax numbers), voice broadcast (in which telephone voice messages are sent to a database of phone

MEDIA	ADVANTAGES	DISADVANTAGES	BARGAINS
Paid Circulation Newspapers & Magazines	• Higher Response Rates	• Expensive • No interaction	• Special Sections/ editions • Stand-by Ads • Classified
Free Papers & Magazines	• Low Cost, Loyal Readers	• Circulation/ response rates may be lower than appearances	• Often negotiable rates • "Deadline" Specials
Radio	• Fastest way to get word out • Demographics targeted • Can be a bargain	• Must run frequently to be heard	• Negotiable Rates • Talk Show appearances are free
TV	• Huge audience	• Expensive • Channel flipping • Timing creates negative first impression	
Billboard	• Long exposure • Huge & captive audience	• Expensive • Poor direct response ability • Negative reactions	• Less traveled areas
Direct Mail	• Effective delivery method	• Low response rate • High waste factor	• Piggy-backing mailers • Non US Mail delivery options • Newspapers
Yellow Pages	• Long exposure • Huge audience	• Expensive • High competition	• Deadline deals
Other Media Fax Broadcast Voice Broadcast E-mail	• Huge audience	• New technology requirements	

numbers), e-mail (where e-mails, which can include text, graphics, and animation, can be sent to a database of e-mail addresses), and streaming video e-mail (a newer technology which goes beyond the flash animation of earlier systems, and which generally requires recipients to have high-speed internet connections).

I have discussed several of these technologies already, and will consider several more of them in greater depth later, but suffice it to say, the same basic considerations apply as in the more conventional media previously discussed in this chapter.

*"It's not what you know...and it's not whom you
know... It's who knows you that really matters!"*
- Jason Hartman

◯◡ Chapter Nine ◯◡
Become a Celebrity

EVERYONE NOTICES A CELEBRITY. People will go out of their way to see them, associate with them, and often, will try to emulate them. Now before you write this chapter off as not being relevant to you because you don't play basketball or act, stay with me for a while. I'd like to share with you some tips on how anyone (even you) can gain some degree of local celebrity status (by the way, don't confuse being a "celebrity" with being a "superstar" - the first is achievable by the average guy or gal, the other isn't). Those of you who have some talent, or if you have something interesting to say, or some particular area of expertise, and you work at developing and promoting it, you really can become a celebrity. In fact, you might even be able to achieve greater celebrity status than the "basic" kind that I'm discussing here.

First of all, as I am sure you are well aware, becoming famous requires publicity because by definition, to be a celebrity people need to know who you are and what you do. The most effective publicity for this purpose typically comes through the mainstream media such as television, radio, and newspapers (and other print media). In the last chapter, I discussed the media in some detail. In this chapter, I'd like to revisit the media and discuss ways they can be used in your quest for notoriety. It should be noted that while media exposure is a great way to develop celebrity status, it isn't the only way. Getting your name and face before the public by direct mail, through newsletters and informational flyers, is also effective in gaining notoriety. Outdoor advertising (billboards, bus stop benches, carwash waiting areas) is another effective way to get people to notice you, as is the use of seminars and workshops, and community involvement in politics, local theater, or charities. Public speaking and publishing a book are also excellent ways to become a celebrity.

TELEVISION AND INFOMERCIALS

THAT'S OVER 100 GUESTS PER DAY!

Getting exposure on television is easier than you think because over 3,600 guests are needed for talk shows and other local and national programs every day. While you can submit your story ideas directly to the station's newsroom, it's the advertising department where you'll find the greatest cooperation and plenty of good ideas (since advertising generates the bulk of a station's revenue, it shouldn't come as a surprise that they will cooperate and suggest ideas to prospective advertisers!). You certainly could generate some attention by personally promoting your product or service through paid advertising spots, but that will usually not get you celebrity status because you will be perceived as "just another ad," although people have achieved notoriety with clever ads and frequent runs. This can be very expensive and probably won't be effective unless you have a memorable ad or an unusual personality.

One of television's most effective marketing techniques is the infomercial, most commonly a fifteen to thirty-minute production that runs on a local cable channel, or at a much steeper price, a network channel, usually late at night. Infomercials can also be short (60 seconds to a minute). Because of the huge audience that television attracts, many successful infomercials have aired late at night, when ad rates are the lowest, and they still reach large audiences. Late-night TV is still relatively expensive, but not as much as you might think. Of course, airtime is not the only expense incurred. There is the rather high initial cost of producing the infomercial. There are a number of very professional production companies that will write the script and produce your infomercial at costs ranging from a few thousand dollars to a half-million dollars or more. In the infomercial business, you usually get what you pay for, but to keep costs down, you can request your local cable company to give you a quote for production costs. Or you can check your local community colleges or high school audiovisual departments to see if they can assist you. High schools and colleges are sometimes good sources of (amateur) talent to handle the production of a short infomercial. Cable television stations might inexpensively produce your infomercial for a few thousand dollars, while college or high school media classes might be willing to do it for the experience or just the cost of film and expenses. Professional studios and agencies would usually be your least desirable choice in terms of cost, but they will produce the best quality infomercial. I personally do not believe that skimping on the production is wise because it is the quality of the script, acting, and production of the infomercial that determines its ultimate success.

The Federal Communications Commission (FCC) requires that cable companies make airtime available for local programming. That doesn't mean they will give you free airtime for your infomercial, but it does mean that you can find significant bargains if you look for them. Television stations usually have downtime when they lack sufficient programming and advertising. Talk with your local cable advertising representative, as well as network salespeople. Always remember that you can negotiate prices for advertising in thirty-minute segments. Stations want and need your infomercial! They hate it when they have nothing but old movie reruns to broadcast. They are almost pleading with you to advertise. If you can make a killer deal, take it. Never doubt the size of the television audience, even at three A.M.!

Your infomercial is a major investment in your business, your product, and your branding efforts. You need not spend a fortune, but you can expect it to cost significantly more than alternatives such as newspaper advertising. One of the main advantages of the infomercial, however, is that it elevates you and your company to celebrity status. When you are on TV, people consider you a celebrity, regardless of what you do on the air. Once the investment is made to produce your infomercial, you can run it as often as you like, and if you have a good script, and a desirable product or service, the results will astound you.

Thirty minutes is a long time to hold your audience's attention, especially in this era of remote controls and 150-channel cable services. In a split second, your audience will switch to another channel if your infomercial isn't sufficiently informative, imaginative, provocative, entertaining, captivating and educational. You'll need compelling testimonials and interesting guests. You'll need to consider how best to present your product, how to create urgency, and how to generate sales via an 800 number that viewers can call to place their orders (no one ever promised you that becoming a celebrity would be easy or cheap).

Another excellent way to market your product or service with an eye toward gaining celebrity status is through shop-at-home television programs. If you have a unique product or service, or if you can package and present it in an interesting way, you may be able to get a shop-at-home show in your local area to carry it. If your product is strong enough, you may even be able to get national exposure. Because they derive their income from the sale of the products presented, these programs have a natural interest in considering your offering. Whether they agree to air it or not depends a great deal on the nature of your product, its packaging and presentation, and the amount of profit they will realize. If they turn you down, ask why. Ask them for tips on how to make your product or presentation more appealing or more unique. On the other hand, if your product is accepted, you're all set. Be careful, however, of extra costs that could make your offering unprofitable. For example, if your product doesn't sell, you may be liable for shipping, returns and/or expensive markdowns. If you're not already a shop-at-home viewer, become one. Study the product offerings, the packaging and the presentation. Notice the pricing structure as well. Remember these programs derive their income from product sales, so they will want a significant percentage of your sales revenue. Be sure to factor this added expense into your pricing.

Let's go back to the media newsroom. If you, or your product or service, is interesting and unique enough, you may be able to get yourself or your product featured on the air as a news item rather than having to buy a paid advertisement. Publicity is far more credible to the viewer than any form of paid advertising because it is not viewed as self-serving. But the trick to getting free publicity is to be newsworthy. Remember that a primary motivation for television producers is ratings. He or she faces stiff competition from other stations, and is always willing to consider a proposal that can give his or her station an advantage over the competition. To obtain this kind of exposure, don't go in with the apparent intention of drawing attention to yourself or your business. Rarely will you get publicity if it seems like you're just looking for free advertising. For example, you could design your pitch as a community service, perhaps involving the perennial safe bets of featuring kids, pets, police, schools, church, hobbies or family activities. Make sure to let the reporter know that you'll be hosting it personally, however. Ultimately, you are doing all this to become a celebrity. Don't go to all this trouble and effort if you are not

REMEMBER THE MEDIA HYPE ABOUT "NEW COKE?" OR DEAN KOMEN'S "IT" TRANSPORTATION DEVICE... OR???

199

getting the personal exposure to help you become a well-known personality!

Note: if you can create a "story" that's newsworthy, then you can offer it to a news channel as an "exclusive" and perhaps get more air time. They are always looking for interesting stories that other stations can't get.

RADIO

You have a much better chance of getting publicity on radio than you do on television. While the overall effectiveness of radio exposure may not be as great as television, it still has impact and can generate significant visibility for you and your product. But as with television, before approaching program directors at radio stations, you must give considerable creative thought to your program idea. In general, AM stations and those with a news or talk format are more open to new programming ideas than are FM and music stations. After selecting a station, to improve your chances of getting on the air, try to establish rapport with the general manager or program director. This is more likely to happen if the relationship is mutually beneficial (we've already discussed the advantages of mutual benefit in the relationship marketing sections of this book). If you have something that the radio station wants, such as advertisers or program sponsors, you will be in a much better position to ask them for something. If you can bring other advertisers to the station, you may be able to offer both programming (your story) and sponsorship (the advertisers), and both you and the station win (and you get the publicity you wanted).

As an example, let's assume you own a real estate brokerage, and you would like to get some publicity on a local radio station. It would be naïve to expect the station to give you airtime if you asked for free advertising, but you may be able to get them to air a how-to-do-it home-improvement program sponsored by your company, and hosted by you. To make your proposal even more attractive for the radio station, offer to do some of the legwork. For example, line up guests for the show: interior decorators, contractors, landscapers, upholsterers, etc. Also, obtain sponsors for your program. Is this a winning situation for the station? You bet it is! It's a double win for you because you foster new and beneficial relationships with area businesses and trades people, while you gain local celebrity status as a radio personality, and have the opportunity to promote your own business.

If the radio stations in your market area aren't agreeable to free publicity or sponsored program scenarios, you may try a different approach - a paid radio infomercial format. This works the same way that television infomercials do, but involves only a fraction of the production costs. Instead of free airtime, you purchase the time in whatever segments you wish - ten, twenty, thirty minutes or more. You interview guests on the show, just as you would if the station were giving you the time, and your show will appear to be regular programming, not a paid commercial.

PRINT MEDIA

Obtaining newspaper stories about yourself or your business requires planning, just as with radio and television. Newspaper feature sections such as the Business, Real Estate, Automotive, or Entertainment sections, offer the best opportunities for getting into print. Rather than simply submitting your idea cold to the "newsroom," where it is likely to get lost or discarded, make sure you become familiar with the publication so as to know who the reporters are that would be most likely to have an interest in your idea. Contact them directly, schmooze them to build rapport, and send them your story idea, photos, or even the completed story itself. The more work you do for them, the better they will like it, and the more likely you are to get a receptive audience when you call them. Don't overlook public relations account executives, who have many excellent contacts!

You may have better luck with the smaller weeklies and free publications in your area than with the daily newspaper. Many smaller publications routinely run feature stories on their advertisers, and may even allow you to write a regular column. If you have such an opportunity, take full advantage of it, but be sure to write interesting and competent columns and feature stories. These publications will usually run a story if it has a "local" angle. If writing isn't your strong point, have someone else in your organization, or an outside copywriter write your material for you. The local publications often have a small staff to produce the content, but they usually appreciate the help if you can do the job yourself.

DIRECT MAIL

Using the mainstream media isn't the only way to get exposure in your community. Direct mail is a sure way to get your feature stories, columns and press releases into the public's hands (whether they read them or not is another matter). Starting with your customer database, the direct-mail method is perhaps the most efficient way of reaching your target customers, and will definitely cost less than a television infomercial or a paid column in a newspaper.

Periodic newsletters are also an effective way to use the mail. ADVO, one of the world's largest direct mail companies, reported recently that in polling direct-mail customers, more than 90% did not include newsletters in the category of "junk mail." Recipients were more likely to think of newsletters as if they were magazines, and they placed a higher value on them.

The most effective newsletters are information-oriented. The more interesting and useful they are, the more likely they are to be read, and thus become an effective sales tool. In addition, newsletters should have eye-appeal and, if possible, involve the reader in some way. Crossword puzzles and contests are two examples of how to make a newsletter interactive. The lead article should be entertaining or informative, certainly not an advertisement. The story should have the appearance of a good newspaper article in its layout, using a creative and attention-grabbing headline, a well-written and compelling first paragraph, with the use of eye-catching graphics and photographs wherever possible. There are several good newsletter-writing software programs on the market, but to give it that "personal touch," you're better off creating something unique yourself. Study the elements of good layout and design, or you may wish to have your newsletter professionally created by an advertising agency or public relations firm. It will be worth the added expense, as you will get much better reader response.

You may even choose to send audio or video cassettes. This is an effective way to speak directly and personally to your target audience, and you can use a more varied approach than is possible with print media, as you can utilize speech, music, product demonstrations, and testimonials. Videos are inexpensive to make and reproduce, and even including the costs of packaging and mailing, they should cost less than sponsoring radio or television programs. Since people are less likely to throw a cassette or video in the trash, partly because the contents are invisible until played (unlike printed "junk mail"), the curiosity factor ensures many people will pop them into their players or VCR's to see what's on them.

Be sure to include the Internet in your overall strategy. Have articles and other useful information on your web site to attract visitors, and be sure it's interesting and timely enough hold their attention (keeping visitors to your website from leaving is often referred to as "stickiness"). Periodically monitor your Internet site statistics to see how many people are visiting, and reading or downloading information and articles. Depending upon your product or service, properly designed and promoted, your website can be one of your most valuable marketing tools.

Frequent visibility in your community, whether in person or through the media, will inevitably get you a certain degree of notoriety. Many business people increase their visibility by offering free workshops and seminars, which can be straightforward and informational, or more elaborate, including refreshments, entertainment, or celebrity guests. Workshops and seminars are excellent ways to interact with your customers and prospects on a face-to-face basis. Whether you are the presenter/speaker, or you introduce a guest speaker, you will rise in stature in the eyes of your audience. To be sure that people attend, keep your customer's needs and interests in mind when you organize your seminar or workshop. Then make sure that your audience leaves with more than they expected. Remember that the occasion isn't a sales pitch, but a way to gain notoriety and credibility. Be well prepared, informative, entertaining, and humorous, but above all, give something substantial to your customers and prospects. Remember that time is your attendees' most valuable commodity, and if you want them to spend their time with you, they must believe that they will receive more value or enjoyment at your seminar than they will receive by watching television, going to the mall, or doing any one of the many other things that they would normally do instead.

WRITE A BOOK

There are very few things that will give you more credibility and notoriety than writing and publishing a book. You're probably thinking that I must be joking - how are you supposed to do something as difficult as write a book? It's not as difficult as you might think.

In the first place, as with any big project, the first step is to break it down into small segments. If writing a book seems like a daunting big task, look at it instead as a series of little tasks. For example, set a goal for yourself to write one page a day, and before long, you will have enough pages for an entire book (remember not to confuse quantity with quality. "A lot of pages" is not the only criteria in writing a book. There must also be valuable content, or no one will buy it or spend the time reading it). Your book does not have to be the size of "War and Peace." Whether fifty pages or five hundred pages, your book can give you celebrity status if it has value to your readers.

It's natural for novices to doubt their capabilities. There are numerous books to help you get started, such as "The Complete Idiot's Guide to Creative Writing." If you are not good with words, you can hire an editor or ghostwriter to collaborate with you to do the actual writing. If you can't find a publisher, you can self-publish your book. There are also many books available to help you with this aspect of the job, such as "The Complete Idiot's Guide to Getting Published." There are many ways to achieve notoriety in this area, but whatever the case, you must actually start in order to get the job done. Remember, whatever your area of expertise, you surely have something interesting and unique to share with the world!

Here are a few more tips. To help you get into the habit of writing, discipline yourself by setting aside time every day to put your thoughts down on paper or your computer. An hour or two a day may yield several pages of copy, or it may yield only a few paragraphs. However much it is, it is something (which is always better than nothing), which you can edit, expand or delete later on. It's important to at least get your ideas down on paper, so you don't forget them. Write about what you know, and make that a cardinal rule. The more involved with and knowledgeable you are about a subject, the easier and faster you will be able to write. "Faking it" will quickly be obvious to your readers. You must be genuine and knowledgeable to be a successful writer.

ROZAKIS, LAURIE E., PH.D. THE COMPLETE IDIOT'S GUIDE TO CREATIVE WRITING, ALPHA BOOKS, 1997.

BYKOFSKY, SHEREE AND SANDER, JENNIFER RAEVE. THE COMPLETE IDIOT'S GUIDE TO GETTING PUBLISHED. ALPHA BOOKS, 1998.

Start with an outline. Briefly, in a few sentences, write down your thoughts for each chapter, or section, of the book. For example, if your book is about how to restore vintage automobiles, divide your book into segments. You may write a segment, or chapter, on how to gather information to ensure authenticity of your restoration work, another chapter on where to find hard-to-get original parts, another on how to restore leather, metal and wood, and another chapter on how to value and sell your restored automobile. I think you get the idea.

Buy some folders and title each as one of your chapters, subjects, or main topics. Keep your eyes open for articles and other information that you can use as part of your research. Put the article in the appropriate folder. Whenever you get a brainstorm, jot it down and put the note in the appropriate folder. If you use photos and other graphics, put these in your folders as well. Soon, the folders will be full of useful ideas and information that can then be incorporated into your chapters. Before you know it, gathering information and worrying about how you will ever fill an entire book will cease being a concern. Your problem now will be to edit out the extra material so your book isn't too long!

If you are not as polished as you would like to be in the areas of vocabulary, grammar and syntax, I would highly recommend the services of a professional editor or ghostwriter. Many work on a freelance basis and will improve the readability of your book for a reasonable fee, which can be based on the hour, the page or the entire job. A good editor will polish the grammar, content, and flow of your book to ensure that it is to commercially acceptable standards. Only after your book is professionally edited should you even consider sending it to a publisher. Poor writing will get you a rejection before the publisher has finished reading page one.

Once your book is written you have several choices in making it available to the public: (1) try to interest a royalty publisher, (2) try to interest a subsidy publisher or sponsor, (3) self-publish it, or (4) make it available as an "e-book" on an encrypted website (whereby readers can read it on-line, or download it and print it out on their own printers, for a fee).

Royalty publishing involves assigning certain rights to the publisher, who will incur the costs of editing, designing the cover, formatting, printing, and marketing the book. While publishers may pay you royalties based on a certain percentage (usually between 5%-9%) of the retail value of the book, after the publisher has recovered all expenses, be aware that expenses can exceed the actual printing costs of the book, and will probably include promotion, advertising, and distribution, in addition to the costs of production. Another consideration is the length of time it takes a publisher to have your book on bookstore shelves. It's usually one to three years, and if you have written time-sensitive material, it may be out of date by the time it's in the public's hands. So how do you find a publisher to whom you can submit your manuscript? One good source of names is a resource book simply called "The Writer." Your local bookstore or library should have a copy. It lists publishers, the type of material they are looking for, and how to submit your manuscript.

CHECK OUT WWW.WRITERMAG.COM FOR ONLINE RESOURCE AND SUBSCRIPTION INFO TO THE WRITER MAGAZINE.

It is always better if you can submit your manuscript by invitation, rather than unsolicited. Book publishers receive so many unsolicited manuscripts that they often do not have the time to even look at them. That doesn't necessarily mean they are not interested in what you have to offer, but that they have plenty of manuscripts to read that they have requested, and they really don't have the time to consider all the others.

How do you get an invitation to send your manuscript? Follow the guidelines that the publisher outlines, either in the reference books, or in response to your written or telephoned request for information. Usually, publishers can tell by reading a one-page summary statement whether they'd be interested in your book. If your manuscript is rejected, don't get discouraged! The odds are heavily against acceptance by a royalty publisher. Many successful authors of blockbuster books were rejected over and over again before finding a publisher. Rejection just comes with the territory!

If your book is accepted, be sure you have adequate legal representation before signing a contract. Typically, publishers will want to buy the rights to your book for a percentage of the sales revenues (royalties). When you sign a contract of this kind, you usually give up ownership of your book to the publisher. This means that your publisher may have all reprint rights, second language rights, movie rights, etc. Chances are, your book will not be translated into fifty languages or made into a movie, so you don't want to kill a deal over unrealistic concerns, but be careful nevertheless to protect yourself. It's always a wise investment to retain the services of an attorney knowledgeable in the ways of the publishing industry when negotiating contracts or agreements. Once signed, contracts are binding and can't be easily changed!

The second publishing option is by *subsidy publisher,* or partnership arrangement. In this scenario, the publishing costs are split between you and the publisher, as are the royalties. For example, you may pay the printing and production costs, and the publisher may pay the marketing and promotional costs. Be careful of this type of arrangement as well. Make sure the publisher spells out exactly what they are going to do with your book (how they will promote and distribute it), exactly how the costs and royalties are to be split, and how and when they are to be paid.

DON'T LET EGO OR DESIRE BLIND YOUR REASON.

Here is a word to the wise: there are numerous publishing scams that prey on anxious and gullible authors. Many authors have fallen into the hands of unscrupulous subsidy publishers who bilk them out of large amounts of money to cover inflated "costs," and then fail to print or adequately promote the book. This kind of scam is particularly common in "ego" businesses, such as writing, acting, modeling, etc. People are so anxious to be famous and successful that they will do virtually anything that is asked of them, including paying exorbitant sums for worthless or unnecessary services. Be on your guard, keep your wits about you, and don't believe everything you are told by people with their hands out about how wonderful, talented, or beautiful you are!

A third option is *self-publishing*. The most important drawback of this approach is that you will personally incur all of the costs involved in producing your book, including cover design, editing, formatting, printing, binding, distribution and promotion. On the other hand, you retain complete control of your book, keep 100% of the sales profits, and you aren't subject to the often misguided whims of publishers who may want to slice and dice your cherished work. There are lots of other details that you must consider that may not be obvious to the uninitiated, such as obtaining copyrights, ISBN numbers (International Standard Book Numbers, which serve as the cataloguing device for all books in print), and bar codes for computer scanning at bookstore checkouts.

While there are publishing consultants that you can hire to help you get the job done right, many authors choose to do it themselves. In my opinion, doing it yourself is the more sensible (and economical) approach if you only intend to use the finished product as a promotional aid in furthering your career. In any case, even if you think you've written the next "Gone With The Wind," be conservative in your publishing cost estimates. It's better to err on the side of too few books printed than have a garage full of books that you can't sell (or give away). If you need more, you can always do a second printing.

The fourth option: you have a real advantage over authors of the not-so-distant past in that you can make your work available via the *Internet*, whereby your book can be posted on your website and read online, or printed out by the reader for a fee charged to his or her credit card. While it is harder to control distribution and prevent piracy of digitized works, the website is a relatively low cost way to market your book. Your website also gives you the ability to offer only selected parts of your book, which can then be used to stimulate interest in buying the actual printed volume, or you can serialize it, offering a few pages each day, or you can sell the book via your website store, and offer on-line ordering via credit card. Be creative in the use of your website - it's a new medium and you can do many innovative things with it.

PUBLIC SPEAKING

The last method that I want to discuss for building notoriety is public speaking, which, while the source of absolute terror for many people, can actually be lucrative and fun, and is very effective in enhancing your celebrity status. It also presents a great opportunity to network with large numbers of people. However, as with the entertainment business, developing a successful speaking career on a large scale is a slow and uncertain process.

It's usually best to start on a local level, such as with civic groups and associations. They are always looking for speakers for luncheon or breakfast meetings, and this will give you an opportunity to gain public speaking experience, though you usually will not be paid for these engagements (you may get a free breakfast, however!). Don't let the limited scale of these appearances lull you into a state of complacency about the quality and content of your presentation. Be prepared. Don't try to fake your way through any public presentation - your audience will not be fooled, and you will risk not only being embarrassed, but you could ruin your prospects for future bookings. Be entertaining, sincere, and most of all, be informative. Give your audience more than they expected. Remember that successful entertainers such as Jerry Seinfeld and Whoopi Goldberg spent considerable time playing the "rubber chicken circuit" and performing in small, obscure clubs, before making the big time.

If you want to expand your speaking to a regional or national level, you should join a speakers' bureau. Speakers' bureaus give you wide exposure and help you obtain bookings, and they also offer your biography and presentation materials to groups and organizations that are looking for speakers for their meetings and conventions. They act as a clearinghouse or broker to help you get in front of larger audiences on a broader geographical scale. Perhaps the best-known speakers' bureau and the one that offers the most prestige is the National Speakers' Bureau. All you need to do is submit a short biography and a recent photo, along with your presentation synopsis. You can find the requirements and address of the Speakers' Bureau on-line at (www.nsb.com).

THE POWER OF RECIPROCITY

In Chapter 3, I discussed important concepts used in relationship marketing and Personal Branding programs. In this chapter, I'm concerned with obtaining notoriety. Both of these topics are interrelated. What, really, is fame but a perceived relationship between a fan and a celebrity? Without ever meeting or personally knowing the celebrity, the celebrity's fans join clubs, collect memorabilia, attend overpriced concerts, etc. If asked, many fans will do nearly anything for their idol. This phenomenon is not a whole lot different than in the relationship between a company and its loyal customers. A loyal customer will gladly act as a *de facto* salesperson for you if you play the game properly.

If you treat your customers well, they will tend to reciprocate. Reciprocity is a by-product of human nature, so it is a very powerful ally for you to use in building your business. For example, if you can enlist your customers in a referral program from which they can derive some personal benefit, you will have all the new business you can handle.

Referral is a process that requires careful nurturing because it involves trust, which must be built gradually over time. You will usually start getting referrals only after the initial rapport-building stage of the customer relationship has been effectively accomplished. The prospect is then much more likely to trust you and your business as your credibility becomes established.

A customer refers a friend because he or she feels genuine trust in, and appreciation for, your product or service. It's a way of thanking you for a job well done, or of doing friends and family a favor. There may even be a sense of obligation - almost as if they owe you additional business. As we have seen, this is what relationship marketing and Personal Branding are all about - building strong and reliable relationships with customers for the benefit of both parties.

Many companies try to stimulate referrals with rewards such as free dinners, or discounts on the company's products. However, the underlying reason most people refer others isn't for such personal gain, but because they feel good about their relationship with you, and they would like others to benefit from a similar relationship.

Rather than giving rewards just to get referrals, always give something extra to your customers to create a sense of abundance rather than the scarcity approach that unfortunately prevails in so many commercial transactions. By that I mean, everyone benefits and feels richer for a well-executed relationship-based transaction in which a state of abundance prevails. In traditional sales, where the company tries to squeeze every last penny out of the customer, and the customer feels ripped-off in the process, a feeling of scarcity prevails.

Percy Ross, a multi-millionaire who gave money to those in need through his syndicated newspaper column, says this about living in a state of abundance: "Giving money away can be compared to tap water in your kitchen sink. When you have the tap on, and water is freely flowing out of the tap, a never-ending supply of water is refilling the line. When it is not on, no water is refilling the line.

That's the way it has been for me. Every opportunity that I touch turns to gold when I am willing to give it away. I have never had such abundance in my life."

Relationship marketing can be looked upon as abundance thinking. It's about opening the tap and allowing others to benefit from your expertise, your talents, and your wealth. When someone gives, with no strings attached, a remarkable energy is released, and the recipient feels an obligation, if not a desire, to reciprocate. When applied to sales, abundance thinking converts the sales process to one based on what you can give to each other, not on what you can get from each other.

People appreciate even the little things. Joann Fisher, president of "Write When U Need It" in Fullerton, California, says that her customers were not returning even with her exceptional service. When she started mailing them personal reminder notes, however, "they came out of the woodwork." She says, "That was an awakening for me. It wasn't good enough to build my business around great service alone; I had to remind people every now and then that I was still here, and that I cared about them. They always came back." Now, she mails out quarterly newsletters, birthday and anniversary cards, and thank you cards. Her customers appreciate being remembered and valued, and they reciprocate with repeat business and referrals.

The *Fairfield Inn* in Buena Park, California, had one of their most successful mailings when they sent cards to their past guests with the message, "In your busy day, take time to relax. Have a cup of tea on us." A tea bag was enclosed. More than four hundred past guests took time to call the Fairfield Inn, just to thank them for their thoughtfulness. A very little gesture had a huge result!

The process that I just described, of building a referral base and maintaining strong relationships with your customers, is frequently referred to as after-marketing, and derives its name from service given after the sale has been made.

If you follow the recommendations in this chapter, I can almost assure you that you will become a star in the eyes of your customers!

*"No matter what accomplishments
you make, somebody helps you."*
- Althea Gibson Darben

∾ Chapter Ten ∾
Schmoozing For Dollars

NOWHERE IS RELATIONSHIP MARKETING and Personal Branding more widely used than in networking groups and organizations, where you have the opportunity to meet people who offer little or no resistance to getting to know you. They are networking for the same purposes you are - to meet other people and grow their businesses. Professional networking groups not only give you expedient introductions to prospective customers, but they give you the opportunity to establish valuable relationships with other entrepreneurs and business contacts that could open doors you may never have noticed were available to you.

When you become involved in networking organizations, don't forget the old rule that giving is as important - actually more important - than receiving. Don't join social organizations or volunteer groups only because of what they can do for you. While you have a right to expect personal benefit, your membership will be short lived and you will not succeed in building meaningful relationships, if it appears that you are motivated only by selfish objectives.

TO GIVE IS BETTER THAN TO RECEIVE.

As you meet people and network with them in meetings, seminars, association groups, conventions and workshops, relate to them from a perspective of abundance thinking. Ask yourself, "What can I do to help this person today?" In a sense, you should operate your business, as you should your personal life, by "giving unto others as they would give unto themselves." This is the Golden Rule of Business Success.

FRIENDS YOU HAVEN'T MET YET

#1 - Always be early. Vince Lombardi, the late great coach of the Green Bay Packers, repeatedly told his coaches and players, "You're late if you are ten minutes early." It pays to be early for networking events not just to get the best parking place, the warmest food, or the best seat - but also because you may be able to meet the event planner and/or the speaker, one-on-one, before anyone else shows up. You should also have an agenda for every networking opportunity you attend, which should start thirty minutes before the event. Fill out and wear your nametag, greet and meet the registrar and the host, and if possible, meet the speaker.

#2 - Be selective. Arriving early will enable you to pick and choose the most productive attendees to meet, those who can provide the best business opportunities for you. You can't meet everyone in a thirty-minute mixer, and you shouldn't even try, so you have to be selective. By arriving early and meeting the key people involved in the event, you may have an opportunity to offer assistance - remember that mutual benefit is the key to relationship building. As others start to arrive, take note of those who may be your most likely prospects. They are the people you are there to meet. A word of caution: in dealing with the event planners, be careful not to be intrusive or a nuisance. The sponsors have probably adequately arranged for everything and may prefer that you remain simply a guest, but a discreet offer of assistance will not be considered out of place. Be considerate and professional, but be alert enough to recognize and meet those who can be most beneficial to you or your business.

#3 - Be productive. Don't waste your scarce time. Power networking isn't about idly chatting with a friend from the office, or monopolizing the time of someone who can be of no value to you. This is an opportunity to meet new people, key people on your agenda. It will probably be more comfortable to spend your time with a friend, but this is neither the time nor the place for that kind of socializing. You need to move out of your comfort zone with the knowledge that everyone there has come to the function for the same reason - to network and meet other people - to meet people like you! Generally, the first person you should meet is the one in charge of registration, for that person is usually one of the most important people at the event - he or she is typically a close associate of the organizer of the workshop or function. If you ask politely and are early enough, you may be able to get an introduction to the organizer - a valuable link to many influential people. *REMEMBER WHY YOU'RE THERE!*

#4 - Be focused. Your purpose in being early isn't to talk about yourself beyond a brief introduction. Try to think of ways you can assist the organizer or speaker. As I suggested, discretely volunteer your services wherever possible with the ultimate objective of meeting key people. For example, if you are a speaker, perhaps you can offer to speak at one of their future events. You will also probably not be the only one to arrive early. The speaker will be early, too. Stay focused on meeting him or her. Don't worry about appearing intrusive. The speaker knows that it is a networking function, and meeting people is why you are there. He or she will likely just consider you a particularly aggressive networker, and may be impressed with your diligence. If you are allowed to assist, that is a real bonus, because you could become part of the "in" crowd, and hopefully get to meet some of the most influential people in attendance.

Many networking
organizations
intentionally
facilitate
developing these
skills. #5 - Be prepared. Most of us are hesitant and awkward about meeting new people. It's one of mankind's most common fears. An effective way to reduce the fear is to prepare a few good opening "ice breaker" comments or questions. Of course, you don't want to sound as if you are reading them to your new acquaintances, so a little practice is recommended. Soon, the questions will become second nature to you as you develop your power networking skills, and they will help you get over the initial reluctance you may feel about meeting new people. Networking functions are easy environments to meet new people, because meeting and schmoozing are the reasons why everyone is there. Everyone else expects to meet you and looks forward to talking to you. Since they probably have the same apprehension in such situations as you may have, they will be grateful for your efforts at starting a conversation with them. It helps to remember that "strangers are friends you haven't met yet."

#6 - No selling. Networking events are not intended to be selling opportunities. Do not try to sell anything when you meet people for the first time. Efforts to sell create resistance and set up barriers that are out of place at a networking function. Everyone knows that selling is the ultimate objective of networking, but there is a time and a place for it - the time isn't during the first few minutes of meeting someone new, and the place isn't at the networking event. Gather information and refrain from actively prospecting. John Naisbitt, author of "Megatrends," defined networking as "the exchange of ideas, information and resources." There is no mention of selling in that definition. Your primary objective at these events

is to make contacts for future business. The contacts you make are
like gold nuggets. Treasure them as if they were valuable objects.

Obviously, it's important that you remember peoples' names,
and for that purpose, you should carry a small notebook with you.
As soon as the conversation with your new acquaintance ends, jot
down his or her name, along with a few mental "hooks" for
remembering the name, and some brief facts about the person.
The unobtrusive personal digital assistant (PDA), such as those
offered by Palm and Handspring, can be a tremendous help here. If
you are able to get the person's business card, the name is already
on it. Just jot down a brief note or two on the back of the card to jog
your memory about the face that goes with the name. If you usually
have difficulty remembering names, as so many of us do, repeat
the person's name during the first few minutes of your conversation
and try to identify a unique characteristic about the person that
you can associate with the name as a mental reminder. Forgetting
someone's name can be awkward, and it sends that person a
message that you didn't care enough about him or her to remember
the name. Besides, you're going to have to contact these folks
afterwards, and you don't want the whole networking experience
to have been wasted because you can't remember to whom you
spoke, or what was said!

Similarly, you want them to remember you. I've been to events
where people I met and wanted to remember did not even have
business cards with them. "I've run out of cards" does not make a
good impression. Cards are cheap. Always have plenty with you!

#7 - Be complimentary. As you become acquainted with someone
new, find something about which to honestly compliment him or
her. This can be a bit tricky because you don't want to appear
insincere or condescending. The compliment isn't intended as
flattery, but as a way of establishing rapport early in the
conversation. It tells the other person that you appreciate him or

her, and enjoy his or her company. To be effective, the compliment shouldn't be trite or superficial, and it should be given honestly and sincerely, even somewhat matter-of-factly. Don't dwell on it. Say it, and move on with the rest of the conversation. The more meaningful the compliment, the stronger the impact. A compliment about someone's dress or suit may be appropriate and appreciated (so long as the dress or suit merits the praise, and actually looks good on the wearer), but a compliment about a capability or achievement, such as outstanding involvement in some public service, would probably have much more impact. If you've offered a sincere compliment, you'll be remembered for it. One compliment that you should always offer at any networking event is to the person or persons who organized the event. Never leave a function without thanking your host or hostess with an honest compliment. A compliment is worth a hundred referrals.

#8 - Stay in control. By asking questions, you initiate and can control the conversation. You can decide what information you receive, and whether or not the person is a contact that you wish to develop. If not, don't waste time with idle chatter. Politely excuse yourself and move on to your next conquest. A pre-planned personal agenda for every networking event helps keep you on track and in control of the conversation. You should try to find out in advance of the event who is coming, and whom you should make an effort to meet. You have a rather brief window of opportunity at a networking event, such as a luncheon, that features a speaker. The only time available to you is the short mixer prior to the keynote address. Once everyone sits down to eat, it's too late to jockey for a seat next to the one person you wanted to meet. You might already be eight tables away. Staying in control allows you to meet this special person, introduce yourself, compliment him or her, listen to him or her, and invite him or her to sit with you. You could spend a year trying to get this close to your prospect by making sales

calls. And you'll never have the barriers to a conversation any lower
than they'll be at that luncheon. Remember that if you initiate the
introduction and the conversation, you have a better chance of
controlling the outcome. Extend your hand first. Be lighthearted
and easy to be around - and don't try to sell anything!

I recently heard a story (source unknown) that told how a new
account executive was advised by his sales manager that he needed
to make at least ten productive cold calls every day. The sales
manager defined "productive" as getting to meet with a decision
maker, and he told the account executive that in order to
accomplish this, he needed to get in the habit of calling on thirty
or forty businesses every day. The manager promised the young
salesman that if he reached this goal during his first week, making
fifty productive cold calls, he would earn a bonus of $500. The
salesman thought about his options. Making thirty or forty sales
calls every day sounded like too much hard work. He knew that
he'd run into many delays, get many objections, and that he'd have
to get around secretaries and receptionists whose job it is to screen
out salespeople. He figured he'd burn out in no time.

Instead, the salesman decided to network rather than make one-
at-a-time sales calls all day long. He obtained lists of local
networking events from the Chamber of Commerce and the
newspaper, and he attended a different breakfast meeting every
morning. Since he was looked upon as a possible new member,
everyone welcomed him with open arms. Instead of the barriers
he would have encountered in the field, making cold sales calls,
the salesman was able to meet many business executives, owners,
managers and other influential people. The first day, the salesman
had collected the business cards of fifteen new acquaintances he'd
met at a *Toastmasters'* breakfast meeting.

The next day, the account executive attended a *Rotary Club*
breakfast that included many bankers, lawyers and professional

people from the downtown area. Once again, he was greeted and welcomed, introduced to everyone present, and the young man was able to make eighteen new acquaintances. The following day, he attended a meeting of the local Democratic Committee and was introduced not only to the membership of more than sixty people, but also met a U.S. senator, who was the keynote speaker.

The week concluded with a breakfast meeting of the Downtown Development Council, a group of influential men and women who had invited the public to attend and offer suggestions on how to re-invigorate the downtown commercial district.

When the account executive met with his manager that Friday afternoon, the manager asked him how the week had gone. "Fine," answered the young man. "I made 163 productive contacts." The manager was surprised, and a suspicious look crossed his face as he asked the salesman for a list of his successful cold calls. When the salesman offered the list, his manager was speechless, and he handed over the $500 bonus.

The point of this story should be obvious. Power networking is a sales tool too few salespeople use effectively to build new relationships or solidify existing ones.

#9 - Watch the calendar. Opportunities to develop new relationships through networking are everywhere. On any given day, in any given community, there are public events going on in religious groups, civic organizations, political groups, historical groups, forums and workshops, hobby and personal interest groups, etc. By doing your homework and watching the events calendars, you should be able to meet literally hundreds of movers and shakers. These events calendars typically list the name of the group, the time and location of the meeting, and a phone number you can call for more information, such as the agenda of the meeting and who might be in attendance. By carefully choosing the events you attend, you will open doors to many valuable new relationships.

Some of the best networking results come from joining a golf
club. You'll find that executives play a lot of golf, and it's a great
casual environment to get to know some important people who
may be otherwise inaccessible to you. If you don't play golf, it's
never too late to learn.

#10 - Plan your agenda. It is important to know who is likely to
attend a networking function so you are able to plan your agenda
around meeting them. There are a number of ways to find out who'll
be there. The most direct way is to call and ask for a list of registered
attendees. If the organization is reluctant to comply with your
request, or simply doesn't know yet who will be in attendance, ask
for the membership chairman's name and phone number. You
should be able to get a list of the organization's members. Indirectly,
this will let you know who is likely to be there, and what companies
or organizations they represent.

#11 - Do your homework. Once you know who will likely be
attending, find out as much as possible about their companies,
which can easily be accomplished by checking recent company
news releases on the company's website. Know about their products
(this information is also available on their websites). If possible,
request that they mail company and product literature to you. Know
in advance what you're going to talk about, and keep the prospect's
interests in mind. What benefit will he or she derive from meeting
you? Remember that your prospect is also at the meeting to meet
new people and network, and if you are not interesting to him or
her, you will be politely dismissed so that he or she can engage in
more productive conversations with others. You'll probably only
get one chance. What is there about your opening dialog with this
person that will pique their interest sufficiently so that they remain
in conversation with you?

#12 - Share your information. Living in abundance is about sharing. "Give, and you shall receive" isn't just wishful thinking. It is a spiritual law that applies to your business just as it does to your personal life. Sharing applies not just to your money or your time; it also applies to information and knowledge. "Giving creates a void that the universe rushes to fill," says Mel Kaufman. If someone gives you something, don't you feel more than gratitude? Don't you also feel like giving something in return? Learn something that will be valuable to your prospect, and you will likely get something valuable in return. Sharing valuable information is the beginning of a rewarding relationship.

#13 - Discard stereotypes. When you network at associations, chamber meetings, civic functions, workshops and conventions, you are operating in a very different environment than if you are calling on a prospective customer at his or her office. Change your paradigm. Throw away the salesman stereotype and wear the hat of a concerned member of the business community looking for a way to attract a major employer to your area. Normally inaccessible executives of the largest companies in the area become simply concerned businessmen, just like you, working toward a common objective. Find a way to help the Chamber of Commerce achieve its business goals and you become a "community leader" rather than a "salesperson." You can then hobnob with influential and important people you probably could not gain access to in a conventional selling environment.

#14 - Make it easier for strangers. Networking events aren't the place to chat with your friends and associates. They will limit your success in power networking by distracting you from the reason you are there - to meet new people, develop new friendships and set up future relationship-marketing opportunities. But there is also another less obvious reason to seek out the company of

224

strangers. That is, they may be uncomfortable and awkward about meeting new people. In an environment that is stressful for so many people, you would be well advised not to ignore those who hang back at the periphery of the crowd. Just imagine how you would feel if you were sitting at a table where everyone knew each other, and no one bothered to talk with you. When you are gregarious and mingle easily, and ignore less outgoing folks, you lower their self-esteem and help to create a stressful situation for them. Sit between two people you don't know, and draw them into a casual conversation. They will be very grateful. To increase your chances for a productive meeting, look at the firm name on the nametags before you sit. Sit by design, not by default.

20 TIPS TO NETWORKING SUCCESS

#15 - Overcome your fear. If you are one of those who would rather be anywhere else but at a social event with a room full of strangers, remember that Emerson said if you "do the thing you fear, the death of fear is certain." For most people, while meeting strangers can be difficult, which is more uncomfortable - sitting beside a stranger without speaking to him or her (silence is certainly not golden in this situation), or breaking the ice and introducing yourself? The best way to overcome a fear is to face it, and practice doing that which you feared. You will soon find that the fear was unjustified. It's never as bad as you expect, and after you've forced yourself to confront your fear a few times and no dire consequences follow, your fear will be history, and the task will thenceforth be easy, maybe even fun!

REMEMBER MY SKYDIVING EXAMPLE?

#16 - Do the work. When you join a public service group, you should contribute to the group. Many people who volunteer are motivated more by the desire to make profitable contacts than to contribute to the cause, but remember that there should be nothing phony about building durable relationships. Many times in this book I have stressed that you have to give before you can receive. So if the group you have joined establishes a graffiti cleanup project for inner-city neighborhoods, guess who should be wielding a paintbrush on Saturday mornings? You, and numerous others, with whom who you will now be in relationships for reasons other than business. The business will come afterwards, as a natural outgrowth of the bond that develops from teamwork, and working toward a common goal.

#17 - Multiply your efforts through your staff. Once you are engaged in power networking yourself, you should encourage key staff members to follow your example at other events. This allows you to leverage your efforts since you can't be in two or more places at the same time. Train them how to network effectively. Role-play in the office before they go out. By having your staff strategically placed at the right events, you are the first to hear of significant developments in your community. Also, allow them (encourage them) to network on company time. After all, the benefits that flow from their efforts eventually come back to your company.

#18 - Follow up on your new relationships. Presume you recently met someone while you were engaged in a volunteer activity who could further your career or help your company's business. You have a clear choice now - take the initiative to nurture the relationship and help it grow, or kill it through neglect. What would the salesman who made 163 new contacts in a week have gained for all his effort if he had never made a follow-up call? If you have networked properly, your new contacts should remember you and welcome your next call. Should your next call be a sales call? Probably not quite yet. At this time, you only have an acquaintance arising from your mutual involvement in an event or group. Wait until the other person invites you to get down to business, either overtly or through body language. You'll know intuitively when the

226

time is right. Your new prospects will buy from you when it is the right time for them, not when it is convenient for you.

#19 - Competition. You can bypass much of the traffic on the busy highway of competition through power networking. Build an overpass by asking questions such as these:

"What does your company do?" Listen carefully and you will learn not only what they do, but you may also learn with whom they do it. For example, you meet the manager of a printing company, and find that his responsibilities include purchasing presses, paper, ink, and related supplies. He is likely to know people at his suppliers whom you would like to meet, and if you foster the relationship, he may make important introductions for you.

"What do you do within your company?" The answer will very quickly tell you whether or not you are speaking with a decision-maker. Even if you aren't, you may be speaking to someone who has access to a decision-maker, and would be an invaluable contact for a future introduction. You may wish to actively pursue this relationship, or maybe you don't, but you are in control by asking the questions.

"Who makes up your target market?" If you are in complimentary businesses (it's probably best in this situation if you are not direct competitors), and their target market is similar to yours, you have the potential for forming an alliance that could be mutually profitable. When you know their target market, you may be able to introduce them to others at the event who it would be beneficial for them to know, thereby establishing new relationships based on trust and mutual benefit.

"How long have you worked at your company?" The answer will let you know if they have influence with many others at their firm. Also, if they have been employed there only a short time, they may need new contacts to further their own careers, and may appreciate your help in introducing them to others.

Think of other questions such as these, which can lead the conversation in many directions. If you wish to take a conversation further, or pursue a particular subject, simply ask more relevant questions. Once you've practiced the art of directing a conversation, it becomes quite easy to converse with a total stranger. Another important point to remember is this: don't become so engaged in trying to think of the next question to ask, that you forget to listen to the answers. The answers, not your own questions, represent the value in this sort of verbal interplay. You can tell your own story later. Even if you don't see an immediate benefit from the contact, pursue it a little further. Developing relationships before you actually need them is often the key to strong relationship marketing.

#20 - Practice abundant thinking. If you practice abundant thinking, you will soon be living a life of abundance. Make it a habit to give others little gifts of a smile, a compliment, or a helping hand. When you practice giving, your day becomes more productive. Obstacles disappear. When you feel sluggish or lacking in energy, get up and go help someone with a problem. And always remember that a gift should be given without strings attached. If you smile at someone and they don't smile back, rest assured that you have brightened up their day in some small way, and the fact that they didn't reciprocate should not discourage you from smiling again.

*"If you continue to prospect and market yourself
when business is good...business will never be bad."*
- Jason Hartman

∽ Chapter Eleven ∽
Building the Better Mousetrap

LET'S LOOK at a few more case-study examples of how the innovative use of relationship marketing and branding can enhance the success of your business.

Saturn, the auto manufacturer, was founded on principles of superior service and high customer satisfaction, and has sought to establish its brand as a different kind of car company. In June of 1999, the company invited 650,000 Saturn owners to its Spring Hill, Tennessee, assembly plant for a factory tour, free luncheon and a chance to win valuable prizes, including several Saturn automobiles. Promoted as the "Saturn Homecoming," the event was carefully planned by Saturn's parent firm, General Motors, to create the impression that Saturn owners are a special breed of automobile owner; members of an exclusive "club." Saturn expected more than 60,000 people to accept the invitation and attend, and hoped to gain valuable feedback from current and former owners to help them relate more directly and personally to their customers. Saturn's philosophy in planning and promoting the homecoming was simple: if you develop a closer relationship with your customers, they are more likely to remain your customers.

In another example of successful relationship marketing, media giant CBS teamed up with MCA Corp. to help MCA introduce a line of casual clothing based on the popular CBS television series, "Northern Exposure." CBS offered to run 30-second commercials at no charge to promote MCA's line of "Northern Exposure"-related sweatshirts and merchandise. This represented one of the first major relationship marketing ventures by a network, offering airtime for the promotion of products from one of its major series providers.

In exchange for the airtime, which was worth $150,000 per series episode, MCA promised to donate $1 from the sale of every sweatshirt to a charity supported by the network, the World Wildlife Fund. In addition, MCA promised to share with CBS the names and contact information of the customers who ordered merchandise. The results of the joint marketing effort more than tripled expected merchandise sales.

The database grew to include tens of thousands of names, which CBS used in a variety of ways, most notably to enhance their ratings status with other (paying) advertisers. CBS was able to use the database of names to convince "on the fence" corporate advertisers to go with CBS rather than another network.

"That promotion was a win for everyone," said then-CBS-vice president George F. Schweitzer. "We were skeptical at first, but what we thought might be a nice way to contribute to the World Wildlife Fund turned out to have a major impact on our advertising revenues."

One of the most innovative ways that companies now use relationship marketing is in raising capital. Going directly to their customers, or to residents in their immediate market areas, companies are now able to float DPOs (Direct Public Offerings) of their stock. Liberalization of federal securities laws has enabled small companies to go public without the expense and red tape of fully underwritten SEC public offerings, through the relatively inexpensive and expedient process of DPO's.

Vermont-based *Ben & Jerry's Homemade, Inc.* originally raised $750,000 from a DPO to finance its first ice cream plant. That early offering enabled the company to grow large enough to float a full-scale initial public offering (IPO) that raised $6.5 million. It also now has hundreds, if not thousands, of loyal ice cream-eating shareholders.

Red Rose Collection, Inc., a Burlingame, California mail order company, went a step further. Not only did the company offer its shares to its 450,000 customers, it also offered a lifetime 10% discount on all its merchandise with the purchase of at least ten shares of the $10 stock. The company got 5,000 shareholders and raised more than $2 million in the offering. Red Rose built long-term relationships with many of its best customers, who, as shareholders, will be unlikely to shop elsewhere. Red Rose president and co-founder, Rinaldo Brutoco, was elated with his customers' response. "I'd much rather give 10% in a rebate to my existing customers than spend a lot of money looking for new ones," he says.

L.L. Bean, the Freeport, Maine, outdoor equipment and apparel retailer, uses relationship marketing in a somewhat different manner. In the 1930's, founder Leon Bean offered the use of a private lake in Freeport, Maine to his customers so that they could test his company's latest fishing gear. His customers appreciated the opportunity to "test drive" the products, and to get "hands-on" instruction in its use before they made a purchase. L.L. Bean has continued the program to this day. *The L.L. Bean Outdoor Discovery School* has trained more than 125,000 people in the proper use of its products.

"The classes helped L.L. Bean distinguish itself from its mail order competitors, and cultivated a very special relationship with its customers," says Jeanie Munger, a marketing professor at the University of Southern Maine. "Bean took away the fear of ordering something new from a new retailer. It made the difference."

Eighteen-year-old Jason Rand credits the Bean Outdoor Discovery School with saving his life when his kayak flipped in white water on the Nantahala River in Tennessee. "At first, I panicked when I found myself underwater and flipped, but because of the instruction I received at an L.L. Bean Outdoor School when I bought the kayak, I remembered quickly how to right myself, and I continued on down the river." Catharine Hartnett, a spokeswoman for the company, says that the company gets thanked often from customers who say that the outdoor schools were very helpful in the safe and proper use of the equipment. "We're very proud of our seven decades of instructional safety," says Ms. Hartnett. "We know we don't have to expend the money for instructors and facilities, but we do it because of a commitment to our customers, a commitment which goes beyond a sale."

In a program similar in many respects to Saturn's Spring Hill assembly plant event, Jeep owners converge on the remote mountain town of Blanding, Utah, for one weekend each year. Roads are few, and once outside of town, quickly give way to dirt trails that snake along steep cliffs and deep valleys. Jeep owners gather in Blanding, and then form a long convoy to nearby Arch Canyon National Park. For two days and nights, they drive their vehicles over some of the area's roughest terrain in an off-road experience known as the "Jeep Jamboree."

The weekend offers Jeep owners a rare opportunity to live the adventures depicted in Jeep commercials. For Chrysler Corporation, Jeep's manufacturer, it is an opportunity to get to know its customers and, it is hoped, win their lasting loyalty.

Building on their success with the original Jeep Jamboree, Chrysler expanded the Jamboree concept and now hosts 33 Jamborees nationwide. One enthusiastic Jeep owner, John

232

Krasnovsky, an air traffic controller from Phoenix, who participated in one of the Jamborees, says, "When you buy a new car, you naturally discount a lot of what dealers say because it's their job to tell you how great your new car is. But when you're out here doing that (as a Jeep Cherokee plunges into a stream), it makes you feel somewhat more confident about the product."

Chrysler justifies the cost of the Jamborees by saying that "all efforts to keep and build loyalty with existing customers are a fraction of the cost of attracting new ones." Chrysler has received an extraordinary level of customer loyalty from participants in its Jamborees.

These are just a few more examples of how relationship marketing is changing the way America does business. It is a common sense approach to successful marketing because it is easier to communicate and build loyalty with former or current customers than to find new ones, and it is far less expensive.

"I'd rather be number one in a small group
than number two in a large group."
- Jason Hartman

❧ Chapter Twelve ❧
Clients for Life

BECAUSE REAL ESTATE is my "game," I'd like to share some of my real estate experiences, and the successful marketing techniques that I've developed. Residential real estate is one of the most people-oriented businesses in the world, not only because it involves a very basic and important part of people's lives - their homes - but also because it represents one of the largest financial commitments most people ever make. Consequently, real estate transactions often involve heightened emotions and lots of stress. Also, since most people only buy or sell their homes a few times in their lives, it is especially important to build lasting relationships with clients if you want repeat business, or referrals.

Creating "clients for life" is a proven way to build a substantial on-going real estate business, rather than merely chasing one quick commission after another. If you earn your living from commissions, this is one of the best ways I know of to say goodbye to unpredictable roller-coaster income.

I believe that there are three basic types of sales agents in the real estate business: part-timers, hot leads seekers, and relationship marketers. The first type comprises the largest group, averaging about two transactions a year (usually buying or selling by relatives and friends). Most of these agents are not truly career-oriented when it comes to real estate sales.

Those agents in the second group enjoy some short-term success from their "hot leads" (frequently referrals from relatives and friends), then falter and eventually leave the business.

The third, and most important group is the "relationship marketing group," or those who enjoy long-term success, with most of their business originating with strangers. These folks are also expert at building effective personal brands.

The first group uses relationship marketing techniques almost exclusively to generate their sales, and they probably don't even realize it! They usually do business with their family and friends, and then only because of their close relationships. For example, a man lists his home for sale with his son, but only because his son is "in real estate," not because he is the most qualified and effective agent available.

The second, or "hot-leads," group enjoys greater success because they actually work at selling real estate. In addition to referrals from family and friends, they have a method and work hard at cold calling, prospecting and selling. The drawbacks of this manner of doing business, however, are that it takes an extended and concerted effort, results in a low level of trust with clients (there is no real understanding of, or commitment to relationship marketing or Personal Branding), requires constant attention - days, nights and weekends, has a low closing ratio, and eventually leads to "burnout."

The third group, professional "relationship marketing" agents, do not sell; they attract business. They are doing what the first group does unconsciously, but they are making a planned and

236

conscious effort to establish relationships with a large number of people. Instead of relying only on relationships that they were born into, such as family transactions, they go out and build many new relationships with total strangers (one of the most effective tools that they use is their Personal Brands).

I liken the relationship-building process to setting up a bank account (I call it a "trust bank account"). Like a conventional bank account, every trust bank account has deposits and withdrawals. The "deposits" include things such as consistent marketing, developing and nurturing long-term relationships, frequent and quality communication with clients, and honest dealings. "Withdrawals" include inconsistent marketing (aggressive effort followed by long periods of nothing done and nothing gained); playing the "numbers game" (throw a whole lot of deals against the wall and see what sticks), lack of communication with clients, and deceitful practices.

THE TRUST ACCOUNT ANALOGY WORKS IN ALL RELATIONSHIPS, BUSINESS & PERSONAL.

Benefits from a trust bank account with a large deposit balance include:

- High credibility with your clients and peers.
- Easier transactions with fewer problems.
- Good will.
- Control over your time.
- Financial security - you are in business for the long haul with "clients for life."
- Lower stress - you can enjoy life more because you have more time and more consistent income.
- Loyal clients - you can travel, or just take time off, and know your clients will not abandon you while you are gone.

The reason I have devoted a whole chapter to the real estate sales business (in which you may have no particular interest) is to illustrate how, in general, effective relationship building can lead to a richer life and greater overall success. In real estate, you are usually just another faceless salesperson selling a commodity-type product. Clients can accomplish their objective of buying or selling property just as effectively with dozens of other agents in their areas. Also, it's difficult to measure the effectiveness of marketing programs over the short run because clients only need your services infrequently - when they want to move, or when their lives change, such as when they marry, have children, divorce, change jobs, retire, etc. But even though people buy or sell their homes infrequently, you need to be remembered when they need you, which is any time and all the time. You can't afford gaps in your marketing program, because in real estate, it's "out of sight, out of mind." You need to be in a long-term relationship with your prospects and clients so you are always there when they need you.

Because of the long time horizon, a significant component of successful relationship marketing and Personal Brand building is faith - confidence that what you are doing will ultimately work. I know an agent who diligently prospected ("farmed") a neighborhood for nearly three years before he got his first listing. It's not unusual to work an area for six months to a year before you get tangible results. As I mentioned before, the process is like growing an oak tree from an acorn. So much time is spent with no visible results, but all the while, the acorn is germinating below the surface, and a little sapling is getting ready to poke through the soil and grow into a sturdy oak tree. Communicate with your prospects and clients regularly every two weeks for six months to a year. Do not expect instant gratification, but you can bank on your relationships ultimately bearing fruit.

On whom should you focus your efforts? Start with your personal sphere of influence, including your friends, relatives, members of your church, civic groups, past clients and old classmates. The benefits of working with this group are its low cost, synergism and a high "trust bank account" balance. You don't have to work as hard to build loyalty and trust with this group because you already have it.

In extending your prospecting efforts beyond your personal sphere of influence, you will find "farming" a geographical area is the simplest and most effective way to go. One benefit of working a geographically defined area comes from the visibility of your "For Sale" and "Open House" signs - your name seems to be everywhere (refer back to Chapter 9 on becoming a celebrity). Your brand name is seen repeatedly every day as people come and go - it's like having many little billboards in your geographical spheres of influence.

Remember that the primary goal of relationship marketing is to become the brand of choice in your neighborhood! That means, when homeowners need a real estate agent, they automatically think of you. Remember that "out of sight, out of mind" should be the basis on which you operate your business.

I have seen agents work long and hard to build reputations and then throw it all away by "resting on their laurels." Once you are established in your geographical farm area, do not become complacent. Do not back off from your aggressive promotional activities. Not only does inconsistent activity create inconsistent results, but also you leave the door open for your competition to move into the gap. If you continue to market yourself when business is good, business will never be bad.

Good results are the natural consequence of "doing things right," and part of doing the right things is to visualize the desired outcome. I have found that top agents know in advance how success will look and feel.

They know that the journey is often more important than the destination.

"The only way to have a friend is to be one"
Oscar Wilde

∽ Chapter Thirteen ∽
Becoming Irresistible

WHAT IS IT that makes some people so appealing, even irresistible? Why do you like certain individuals without ever meeting them in person? Is their personal magnetism a natural gift, or is it something that can be learned? In this book, I have sought to show you how important it is to form emotional bonds with your clients and prospects, and to create lasting relationships that inevitably lead to repeat business over long periods of time. I have also discussed ways to become somewhat of a celebrity in your area. What I would like to discuss in this chapter is a few ways for you to develop your people skills so as to make yourself more attractive to others, on both a conscious and subconscious level. To be most effective at Personal Branding and relationship marketing, and building your business, you should work on enhancing your personal charisma so that people enjoy dealing with you, and want to buy from you.

I personally believe that the majority of factors that make a person charismatic are things that can be learned, or enhanced, and which can become a fundamental part of your personality.

While it's certainly true that individuals who have natural charisma have a certain inherent personal "magnetism" that is hard enough to define, much less learn, but that doesn't mean you can't improve your charisma. For example, if you are not naturally creative in the arts, you can't learn how to become a Michelangelo or a Mozart. But even if you are not a naturally great artist or musical genius, you can learn to become a very good artist or musician, and the more you practice, the better you will get. Similarly, while you may not be as naturally charismatic as famous personalities like Mother Theresa, Mahatma Gandhi, or John F. Kennedy, you can become more than you already are by learning and practicing a few basic principles.

Earlier, I stated that the best way to eat an elephant is one bite at a time - in other words, a big, complex job can best be tackled by breaking it into a number of small, simple tasks. Similarly, the best way to accomplish a complex change in your life is one small step at a time. I'm going to discuss a number of charisma-building steps, and just like eating an elephant, they should be digested one step at a time. If you try to bite off more than you can chew, you may choke, and quit eating before realizing the full nutritional benefits of the banquet. Since many of these suggestions involve stepping out of your comfort zone, you should practice them one at a time until you are comfortable with the change, and it becomes a natural part of your personality and behavior. Then you can move on to the next step.

Step Number One, the very threshold for developing charisma, is to genuinely like people. If you don't like people, the rest of this chapter may help, but you will not become truly charismatic. If you like people, you are more than halfway there!

PEOPLE WILL NATURALLY LIKE YOU IF YOU LIKE PEOPLE.

How, you might ask, are you going to learn to like people if you really don't? Since attitudes tend to be contagious, you can start your transformation by associating with people who like people. Their behavior will demonstrate how they interact with others, and

242

if you mimic their behavior, you will start to experience the positive reinforcement that comes from people liking you. Generally, since people like people who like them, you will start to develop warm feelings for others, since you will like the feeling that comes from being liked. If you make this a daily exercise, you should eventually feel more kindly toward everyone. Also, don't pre-judge, or decide in advance, that you won't like someone. Give everyone an equal opportunity to be liked by you, based on the relationship that you will work to build.

The next step is to be non-judgmental of others. Remember that there are few, if any, universal truths as far as attitudes and beliefs are concerned, and just because you think your way is the only way, doesn't mean that everyone else has to agree with you (just as I'm sure you don't agree with everyone else all of the time). As soon as you come to the realization that what you believe to be true is largely a figment of your imagination, and the imaginations of those who trained you and indoctrinated you with your belief system while you were young and impressionable (such as your parents, teachers, clergy, etc.), you will be in a position to accept that what others believe is just as valid as what you believe. Without even knowing you, I can state unequivocally that you are not right all of the time! When you stop judging others and rejecting their points of view, you will have greater respect for them, and start to like them as fellow humans, and find diversity of opinion stimulating rather than threatening or offensive.

Next, don't be argumentative or easily irritated with others. When you are confrontational or argumentative, you instantly create a barrier between you and your "adversary." That sets up a "vicious cycle" which results in your not liking the other person, the other person not liking you, and a wall of anger, distrust and dislike will develop between you. If you repeat this process often enough, you will eventually have an argumentative and irritating personality that will turn other people off, and you will not only dislike and have contempt for people, but your chances of becoming charismatic will decline to precipitously close to zero.

Another important step is to not take yourself too seriously. Once you adopt a less stern and more humorous view of life, and of the world in general, you will find that people enjoy your company and consider you much more attractive. The most powerful tool in your charisma toolbox is humor. If people with whom you interact leave the conversation laughing (hopefully, they are laughing with you, not at you), you have them on your team. One of the key tricks to becoming charismatic is to be light-hearted, humorous, and entertaining. Most people "lead lives of quiet desperation," as Thoreau once said. If meeting you brightened their day, they will not only be grateful to you, but will leave with your occupying a warm spot in their hearts. No one likes a sourpuss!

Suppose it is one of those rare days when you are not in a good mood. How can you be humorous and cheer others up if you aren't feeling cheery yourself? In general, unless you are a very good actor or actress, others will sense your depression or lack of enthusiasm and they will try to avoid you (the last thing they want is to increase their own misery by being around you). So, assuming you are not clinically depressed (if you are, do yourself the biggest favor of your life and seek professional help. Millions of normal, highly functional people consider Prozac® their best friend), work at maintaining a positive attitude. Associate only with happy, positive, "winning" people, and avoid whiners and losers ("It's better to be a winner than a whiner" - Jason Hartman). You can help yourself get out of a bad mood by watching funny movies and television shows, or reading uplifting and motivational books, or recollecting the "wins" in your own life and the progress you've made in achieving your goals. Depressing or violent material, and bad news in general, sets the wrong tone. If there's bad news in the world, don't sit for hours on end in front of the television, watching the terrible images and listening to the sad details over and over again. That just reinforces negative feelings until they overwhelm you. Buy a few joke books, memorize a few good jokes, and practice telling them until your timing and delivery is natural. (Stay away from off-color jokes and other tasteless or offensive material. While you may think "shock jocks" like Howard Stern are hilarious, that is not a universal opinion, and you don't want to offend your audience). Remember that professional comedians usually don't improvise their material...their act is memorized and rehearsed until it is natural and polished. If they can earn a living by telling the same jokes over and over again, you can use your material repeatedly as well (but not to the same audience). By learning to be humorous, you can fake it if necessary, and appear happy and uplifting even when you don't feel that way (an interesting thing will happen if you fake being happy when you're not: you'll actually make yourself happy).

Closely associated with humor is spontaneity, the quality that makes a routine encounter with you an adventure. Spontaneity frees you and your audience from the tedium and predictability of the status quo. It also allows you to be more adaptable to new situations and more flexible and creative in the ways you analyze and solve problems. Your ability to handle the unexpected will make you much more appealing to those who become frozen with fear at the prospect of unpleasant surprises and unplanned-for problems. You will become their savior, and they will seek your counsel in times of stress and distress.

Try to become like the Rock of Gibraltar in the face of unfamiliar situations and approach them as exciting challenges rather than as numbing threats. Become a risk-taker rather than a risk avoider. Remember the old cliché, "nothing ventured, nothing gained." If you keep your ship moored at the dock, it won't sink. Neither will it take you anywhere. It will be essentially useless, and sitting safely in port certainly isn't what it was built to accomplish. If you do nothing, if you take no risks, you can't expect to accomplish anything of significance. When others see you in the vanguard, sword in hand as you vanquish the scary dragon, your charisma quotient will soar!

So far, I have been discussing things to do to become more charismatic. Now I'd like to suggest some ways to be.

Make a list of people whom you consider charismatic. Write the names of your "Top Ten Charismatic Individuals of All Time" and jot down after each a few of the things that in your opinion made them outstanding. When you are finished, see if there are any common threads running through your list. Are they among the so-called "beautiful people"? Are they especially smart? Energetic? Well-dressed? Young? Old? Male? Female? Political leaders? Entertainers? Sports figures? Great communicators? I think you will find that there are very few easy categories that allow you to define "charisma," or to identify those who are or will be charismatic. Your list will probably be "all over the lot," as they say.

When asked, many people would tend to define charismatic individuals as taller, younger, smarter or, in general, usually physically attractive. Yet, such famous people as Mother Theresa, Napoleon, Ronald Reagan, Winston Churchill, and Adolf Hitler all fall outside of these easy categorizations. Mother Theresa surely wasn't young or pretty. Napoleon wasn't tall. Reagan was no glamour boy, Churchill wasn't an Adonis, and Hitler was evil incarnate. Yet all would be considered charismatic by even the most jaded observer.

So, how do you go about identifying those traits that increase charisma, so you can practice them and become more charismatic yourself? I believe that common sense is your best guide here. Seek people who appeal to you as examples. People that appeal to you probably appeal to most others also, as human nature is basically universal. So write down those traits that you find appealing and adopt them as your own. For example, let's consider physical appearance.

Wouldn't you agree that a well-groomed and tastefully dressed person is more appealing than someone who is slovenly and carelessly dressed? I think you would! So learn a few basic rules of tasteful and appropriate dress...what goes together (stripes with plaids?), what's in good taste (short shorts at religious services?), what's appropriate (jeans at opening night of the opera?). While you have been taught that you shouldn't judge a book by its cover, the fact of the matter is, we all judge books by their covers. We judge people by their clothes, outward appearance, and possessions. Unfair and superficial though it may be, that's just the way it is and we might as well accept it, live with it, and use it to our advantage. Most important, remember that you usually don't get a second chance to make a good first impression, so plan on making a good first impression all the time, not just on special occasions or in specific situations. Your charisma must always be apparent, so that it is immediately perceived by those who meet you for the first time, and so that it doesn't seem artificially "put on" for special occasions.

If you are sartorially challenged, pick up a copy of the classic book by John T. Molloy, "New Dress for Success" (Warner Books, 1988), or "New Women's Dress for Success" (Warner Books, 1996). Success goes beyond merely being successful in your business dealings - it also includes success in all your relationships. You can learn much useful information from Molloy's books, and other books of that genre. If you find it difficult to transfer the advice in the books to actually purchasing appropriate clothes at the store, ask for assistance from the store's salespeople, or hire a professional wardrobe consultant. In either case, be prepared to spend money, and don't skimp! You are better off buying just a few tasteful, stylish, high-quality (generally "expensive") garments that fit properly and make you look your best, than numerous lesser-quality and poorly fitted (generally "cheap") items. Do not trade off quality for quantity. In the long run, a high-quality, classic wardrobe will actually be

MOLLOY, JOHN T., NEW DRESS FOR SUCCESS, WARNER BOOKS, 1996.

less expensive than a cheap, faddish one. Your clothes will last longer, look better, and not go out of style in a year. You should always try to look your very best.

Once you have the best wardrobe that you can afford, your next task is to work on improving the person inside your clothes. To be charismatic, you should exude health, physical fitness and energy. Quit smoking. Improve your diet. Get rid of that excess flab. Exercise. Take up Yoga. Get enough sleep. Breathe deeply and take time to smell a few roses. Very few (if any) charismatic individuals come across as weak, tired or bored. You don't have to actually be tall and handsome, or ravishingly beautiful, but if you stand tall, walk with confidence, and act with authority, you will be perceived by others as tall, confident, etc. Another thing to add to your repertoire of charismatic characteristics is a smile! Yes, the most powerful way to communicate your warmth, friendliness, and general charisma is through a warm, sincere smile!

I have come to the conclusion that much of what makes people attractive is their ability to make those with whom they interact feel as if they are the most important people on earth. Charismatic people don't belittle, don't annoy, don't patronize, don't destructively criticize or pre-judge. What they do is make people feel better after they interact than before they met each other. It all goes back to what we have been discussing throughout this book - building mutually beneficial relationships.

I have compiled many of the components of charisma in the following list. I suggest you not only read and understand it, but also breathe it in and make it a part of your being. Your life will never be the same!

50 STEPS TO PERSONAL MAGNETISM

1. Improve and maintain your health, both physically and mentally.

2. Look in the mirror and try to see yourself as others see you. It can be very helpful to watch videos of yourself, or carefully scrutinize candid photos. Notice your clothing, facial expressions, haircut, bearing, etc. Are you projecting the image you want to project? Ask friends for their honest opinions of your appearance, demeanor and style (promising them you won't be offended by their candor).

3. Don't forget to include your auto and home in your self-examination because they convey many overt and covert messages about who you are (sporty, stodgy, faddy, individualistic, practical, etc.)

4. Don't delude yourself into thinking you look better than you actually do. There is room for change and improvement in everyone.

5. Develop a high-energy style, and always appear enthusiastic. However, don't make people nervous by being frenetic or manic. Pace yourself.

6. Be an optimist. People avoid "downers."

7. Learn the fine points of non-verbal communication ("body language"). Practice the things that are helpful, and work to eliminate those things that hurt you in your dealings with other people.

8. Remember to make eye contact (you'll seem more sincere), but be careful not to "stare," or make others feel uncomfortable.

9. Develop a firm, but not a knuckle-crunching, handshake. Shake hands long enough to convey warmth and sincerity, but don't hang on too long - know when "enough is enough" (also, be careful not to hurt people with smaller hands, or those with arthritis).

10. Maintain a comfortable distance from people you don't know well. Respect their personal space and don't crowd

them (don't stay too far away, however, or you will appear standoffish and unapproachable).

11. Maintain a calm demeanor. Agitated people are contagious and unnerving. Charismatic people make others feel better, not worse.

12. Be sure that your conversations are not monologues. Involve others by asking questions and then listening carefully to their answers. Show sincere interest in them and in what they have to say.

13. Don't "multi-task" during your conversations - that is, don't do other things, like reading mail or sending e-mails while talking to people. It is not only very rude, but it interferes with your ability to make people feel that meeting and talking to them is the most important thing that you have to do at the moment. Don't make them feel like they are interrupting something more important.

14. Practice remembering names, and call people by name whenever possible. It shows you care about them, and that you recognize their uniqueness. In a similar vein, remember important dates like birthdays and anniversaries, and wish people well on the important days of their lives.

15. Use humor frequently, but be sure it doesn't offend. People love to be around other people who make them feel happy. Practice your delivery, and watch videos of professional comedians. Concentrate on their demeanor and style, and try to adopt those characteristics that fit your personality. Be careful that you don't become a clone of someone else, however. Develop your own unique style.

16. Focus your conversations. Be brief and to the point. Don't bore your audience with long-winded comments or rambling answers to questions. Don't be a verbal machine

gun - slow down so others can grasp what you are saying, and perhaps get a word in edgewise.

17. Practice what you preach. Walk your talk.

18. Sincerely compliment people when they look good, or successfully complete a task, or when they say something special. But don't be syrupy, condescending, or overdo it.

19. If you must critique someone, don't be destructive or hurtful. Always criticize in a way that conveys that you want to help, not belittle, demean or hurt the other person.

20. Be courteous and respectful of others at all times. Remember that their opinions count.

21. Be punctual. When you are late, you convey the message that the other person's time really doesn't matter to you, and you do things to suit yourself, in your own good time.

22. Be flexible, and be willing and able to adapt to others' needs, or to unexpected or unusual circumstances.

23. If something irritates someone, don't do it. If something pleases them, do more of it.

24. Don't appear to be too taken with yourself. You don't want to seem conceited, and you don't want to sound bombastic, pedantic, or preachy. Don't be a know-it-all. You're probably not as wonderful as you think you are, anyway. Let others come up with some of the answers to questions and solutions to problems, even when you think you already know them.

25. Don't try to be what you're not. Know your limitations, and don't be afraid to admit that you don't know something, or can't do something. Don't try to seem like an authority on subjects you know little about, but speak with authority on those things you do know about.

26. Don't always be the first to jump in and take charge of new situations. It's good to show leadership, but let others make some of the decisions and take some of the actions. It's the difference between being a leader and a commander.

27. A little self-deprecating humor goes a long way toward breaking the ice and making you approachable, warm, and human. Don't take yourself too seriously, but be careful not to make yourself look foolish, either. You want people to laugh with you, not at you.

28. Be patient, and don't jump to conclusions too quickly. You don't have to be first, or right, all of the time. Get the facts and think before you speak.

29. Don't dwell in the past, regretting mistakes made or opportunities missed. Don't worry about, or fear future events that may never come to pass. Do not sacrifice your present to things over which you have no control. Carpe diem!

30. Never try to take advantage of others, or exploit their weaknesses.

31. Don't let your own shortcomings hold you back. Try to turn weaknesses into strengths through a positive attitude and diligent practice, and emphasize your strengths to compensate for shortcomings over which you have no control. Mother Nature may not always be "fair" in the cards she deals, but you do have free will to overcome the bad cards in your hand.

32. Don't be flippant, nasty, sarcastic or caustic.

33. Learn the art of subtlety; don't make your points with a sledgehammer.

34. Don't be evasive. Give people a straight and honest answer when asked a question, or for advice. If you don't know, say so.

35. Speak clearly, use proper grammar, and develop an extensive, but not pedantic, vocabulary. Learn to verbally paint pictures in the minds of those with whom you converse. People judge you by your oral communication skills. Above all, remember the primary purpose is to convey ideas, so don't be difficult to understand.

36. Learn to write clearly, cohesively, and with proper form. Take a few writing classes. As with oral communications, people also judge you by your written communication skills.

37. Read more, and broaden your scope. Charismatic people are perceived as being worldly and widely read. Others should consider you a resource that they can look to for advice and counsel.

38. Write a personal constitution, or "mission statement," to define and give substance to your values and goals.

39. Discuss your feelings with others. Don't give the impression that you are "bottled up" and unapproachable (on the other hand, don't become a "motor mouth" and talk on and on about yourself, or burden others with your problems).

40. Be aware of others and their interests. Share their interests, and put them ahead of your own. Ask questions and listen attentively to the answers. Show that you care.

41. When you make formal presentations, don't try to "wing it." You'll look unprepared and possibly incompetent. Be prepared and rehearse. Know what you are going to say, but don't try to memorize it - be sure your delivery sounds natural, and flows smoothly. You want to look like a person, not a robot.

42. Join a Toastmasters' Club in your area. Effective public speaking is one of the best ways to increase your

charisma. You may also make important contacts with other members of the club.

43. Think before you speak. Be careful not to offend, and don't promise anything you can't or won't deliver. Always remember that once words leave your lips, they cannot be retrieved (take to heart the World War II-era slogan, "Loose lips sink ships"). Do you think when the judge instructs the jury to disregard inadmissible evidence or inappropriate testimony that what they have seen or heard has no effect on their verdict?

44. Be conscious of annoying mannerisms, and make an effort to eliminate them. Such mannerisms can be verbal or physical (such as repeatedly saying "uh," or cracking your knuckles).

45. Learn negotiating techniques. Learn how to get what you want without alienating others by creating "win-win" situations.

46. Be consistent and reliable so that people know what to expect when they deal with you. You are a brand, and your brand must stand for something.

47. Make it obvious to others that you truly enjoy meeting and interacting with them, and that you actually like them.

48. Be true to yourself. If you aspire to be a mountain climber, then climb a mountain. If you constantly try to pound a square peg into a round hole, you will create stress and unhappiness in your life, and others will pick up your negative vibes and shy away from you.

49. If you are excited about your life, others you come in contact with will become excited about their lives, also. Excitement and enthusiasm are contagious.

50. Adopt the Nike shoe company's philosophy and JUST DO IT!

While it is unlikely that the great leaders of history became 50 STEPS TO
charismatic by reading a few books and taking a few seminars, PERSONAL
you must keep in mind that everything is relative. Don't be MAGNETISM
discouraged because you don't think you could ever become a
Winston Churchill. All you need is to be a little better than the
competition to come out on top. Use all my suggestions, or only
some of my suggestions, and you will be pleasantly surprised by
the way your life will change!

Please visit our website

WWW.BRANDOFCHOICE.COM

for a **FREE** newsletter
and additional information on:

- Jason Hartman's Personal Coaching Program

- Booking Jason Hartman for Public Speaking engagements

- Ordering additional copies of this book and other Hartman Media Company Publications

A Few Words In Closing

I sincerely hope you have gotten value out of this book.

Clearly, nothing that I have presented here is rocket science, and there is no reason for you to delay in getting started applying the principles discussed in these pages. I have profited greatly in my own life by using these techniques, and judging from my own experience I know they work. I encourage you to make a commitment to step out of your comfort zone and give them a try.

Whether you want to improve your business, or your personal life, the bottom line is: it's all about relationships. If you learn and apply the secrets of creating and nurturing relationships, your life will blossom with new opportunities. Your biggest task will then be to decide which ones to seize.

OK, enough talk. Now get out there and go for it!

Appendix 1

Real-Life Brands of Choice

THROUGHOUT THIS BOOK, I have tried to show how you can magnify your success, both in business and in your personal life, by building meaningful relationships with your clients, customers, and friends and by promoting yourself so that you become a Personal Brand. I've also stressed the importance of goal setting, and of developing a passionate commitment to your goals. I believe that the path to achievement of your life's objectives is often anything but a straight and smooth path. It can be filled with potholes and blocked by brick walls, it meanders through twists and turns, and has frustrating dead-end detours. To get to your destination, you will have to climb out of the potholes, find ways around the brick walls, waste time on twists and turns, and backtrack from dead-ends to seek another route. But, *c'est la vie* ("that's life" for those of you who speak English as your only language).

On occasion, people have come up to me after a speech, or while I'm talking with them in a social situation, and they've said something to the effect that "what you say may be true for some people, but aren't those people rather rare, and how can an average

259

guy like me ever be exceptional?" That gave me pause, and I started to think about the people that I work with every day in my real estate office. I don't have a very large office, so there aren't that many people in my sample population. I thought of two among those few people who agreed to share parts of their lives with you as examples of how common people can do uncommon things. There are also others in my small office who have done exceptional things, such as the woman who emigrated from Hungary to escape a tyrannical regime, and who had been a competitive swimmer on the Hungarian national swim team.

The point of this is that greatness often comes in plain packages. If you believe that you can do bigger and better things with your life, and are willing to pay the price and make the effort, you can be anything you want to be and achieve anything you want to achieve!

MIKE DUNN

When you first meet Mike, you would probably think that he's an average quiet guy with a nose-to-the-grindstone approach to life and business. "Charismatic" is not a word that comes to mind. Neither is "superstar." But the more you get to know Mike, the more you realize that he is indeed an exceptional person, who has accomplished exceptional things, from whom important lessons can be learned.

When Mike was still in grade school, he decided he wanted to become a major league baseball pitcher. Of course, lots of kids have that dream, but unlike most kids, Mike actually did something about it. He watched lots of baseball on television, but not just for the casual enjoyment of it - he carefully studied every pitch that his pitching idol, Nolan Ryan, made for form and style. Then he went outside, set up a paper strike zone on the wall, and practiced pitching as he had observed Ryan pitch during the televised game.

260

Mike practiced over and over, day in and day out, until he was a star pitcher by the time he got to high school.

Unfortunately, he had an accident along the way, and cut a tendon in his pitching hand. At first, Mike was disheartened, and the thought of quitting briefly crossed his mind. But his high school baseball coach got him back on track, saying, "Mike, you're half way up the fence. You can turn around now and go back down, but then you'll have to climb half way up again just to get back to where you are." So Mike decided to continue climbing instead, rather than feeling sorry for himself and giving up his dream. Without missing a beat, he resumed practicing his pitching - with his left hand, until his right hand had healed sufficiently.

When I asked Mike why he hadn't become a major league pitcher, he said that after winning a baseball scholarship to college, he thought he could simply rely on his past achievements and that his future success would be assured. Unfortunately, he had deviated from his dedication to keep practicing and to never lose the competitive edge. It was an expensive lesson, which he later applied to his real estate business - he now never takes his success for granted. Besides, he says, his fastball was "only 84 miles per hour," and he wasn't able to attract the attention of the scouts who could get him into the majors.

He had other dreams, one of which was to coach and mentor other kids who loved the game. As soon as he was out of school, Mike established a baseball camp, with which he is still actively involved to this day.

To reach his high financial goals, Mike decided to apply the persistence, determination and mental toughness he had learned in his sports training to sales, and that is how he became a star sales agent at my real estate company.

I asked Mike to share his philosophy, and he made the following comments:

- Mike asserts an unwavering faith in the long-term achievement of his carefully thought-out goals. He does not accept failure as an outcome.

- Mike has an unusual amount of personal discipline and the ability and willingness to delay gratification so that he isn't diverted from his long-term goals by short-term pleasures.

- Mike prides himself on having the mental toughness needed to do the things others don't want to do. For example, he spends two to three hours per day, every day, no exceptions, prospecting by phone, making cold calls to his farm area.

- Mike never forgets the basics, and he is always practicing, and repeating the things that work, just as he did after watching Nolan Ryan pitch.

- Mike never lets his ego stand in the way of doing the correct thing, and he is always willing to listen to others and change what he does if he sees that another way is better than his way.

- Mike believes that there is no "magic pill" to achieving success, which only comes with hard work, dedication, persistence, and faith. Often, the mundane, least glamorous approach is the best choice - "the monotonous repetition of the basic fundamentals," as Mike explains it.

- Mike never stops learning from others. He is always willing and anxious to ask people who are successful what they do, and then he does it, too. Mike believes that the same actions will get the same responses.

- Mike believes that much of life is a numbers game. The more he does, and the less deterred he is by failures, the more success he expects to have. He points out that even the best baseball players only succeed in getting a hit approximately 3 times out of every 10 times at bat. If they let the 7 out of 10 failures deter them, they would surely quit the game.

- Mike does not focus on the past, or agonize over past failures, since that would just hold him back from achieving a successful future. Whenever Mike made a bad pitch, he walked to the back of the mound, picked a blade of grass and threw it toward the infield. The blade of grass was symbolic of the last bad pitch, and by discarding it, Mike was able to throw the next pitch with a "blank slate." He says, "If I dwelled on the last bad pitch, I never could have made a successful next pitch."

- Mike says he often "talks to God" whenever he's faced with a difficult situation, failure, or frustration. He starts his conversation with, "OK, God, I see you're testing me again. But I'll surprise you, because you're just going to get me to try harder. Once again, I'll pass your test!"

- Mike is generous with his clients, and keeps in contact with them through monthly lunches, dinners, or giving them tickets to sports or social events.

- Mike says always be creative. From his slogan "Call Mike and it's a Dunn deal" to his extensive use of voice broadcast, Mike works hard to become, and stay, his clients' Brand of Choice. A little promotional gimmick he likes to use is to voice broadcast a joke...minus the punch line. Instead, Mike says "if you'd like to hear the punch line, call me at _____." It works like a charm!

STEFANIE MEURER

Stefanie is one of those unusual women who stands apart from the crowd. The energy in the room changes when she enters. She always looks great, and exudes confidence, intelligence, and style.

As if that weren't enough, she speaks with a captivating Australian accent. You can't help but notice her.

But lasting success in the real estate business requires more than mere image, and Stefanie is well aware of that. While she does not hesitate to capitalize on her natural attractiveness, she never stops working to improve her business acumen and her sales techniques. When I asked Stefanie to share some of her experiences and business methodology for this book, I noticed many similarities between her and Mike Dunn. For example, like Mike, Stefanie did not hesitate to strive for lofty goals. As a child, she dreamed of winning a world-class beauty pageant, and through diligence and dedication to her goal, she realized her dream, winning several important competitions to become a contestant in the Miss World competition, representing Australia.

Another of Stefanie's life-long goals was to emigrate from Australia to America. However, she soon discovered that that was easier said than done. It took Stefanie ten years to realize that goal. It was only by building another career in the travel industry that she was able to achieve the financial stability needed to come to America.

Stefanie loves to travel, and through employment with Qantas Airlines, she became familiar with many cities and tourist destinations around the world. She used her knowledge to become a successful tour operator. Not only did this gain her entry to the United States, but travel also gave her an extensive familiarity with other cultures, and as a result, she was able to appreciate and relate to a wide variety of clients when she later became a Realtor®.

Here are a few of Stefanie's many suggestions for a successful and satisfying career:

- Stefanie never allows herself to "get boxed in" - she always maintains a high level of flexibility and creativity. She believes that there are many roads to success, and the road she happens to be on may not be the best route. She does not hesitate to change routes or direction if circumstances warrant a change.

- Stefanie believes that her best investment is in herself and her own business. "So many agents think that success will just happen, and that they don't have to spend money on self-promotion. I believe that my name, my image and my personal brand are essential to my success, and if I don't believe in myself, and invest money building my business, why should my clients believe in me?"

- Stefanie is a master at networking. She is by nature an unusually social person and has many friends ("including many ex-boyfriends"). She tries to stay on good terms with everyone, and never misses an opportunity to weave her personal life into her business dealings. Many profitable transactions have grown from her many personal relationships. She frequently includes clients in her social activities so that clients become friends, and many referrals have resulted.

- Stefanie carries no grudges and has no regrets, and she never lets past disappointments hold her back from realizing a brighter future. "I can't change the past. What's done is done. I move forward from here regardless of what might have been. I refuse to let what has already happened, and what I cannot change, hold me back by becoming an albatross around my neck," she says.

- Stefanie, like Mike, stresses the importance of knowledge and constant learning. Stefanie believes that in an ultra-competitive business, those with the most knowledge will prevail.

- Stefanie stays in touch with her clients constantly, using her detailed mailing database to send cards and appreciative gifts when appropriate. One of her most appreciated and unique "gifts" is the woman who cleans her home, whom she "gives" to special clients for a week, free of charge.

- Stefanie uses what she learned from her beauty contest days to her advantage whenever possible in her business. "Don't overlook what you have learned through blood, sweat and tears in your earlier years. It's an integral part of your overall education and preparation for your later life," asserts Stefanie.

- Stefanie always tries to put herself in her client's shoes, and to see as they see, and feel what they feel. She believes that successful relationships, especially in sales, are built by helping people achieve their dreams. "I don't sell houses - I sell dreams," Stefanie says.

- Stefanie has carefully defined her Personal Brand as the "Realtor to the Stars." She builds her image by emphasizing flamboyance and a glamorous style, and maintains a "high profile" whenever she's in public.

Appendix 2

AutoMagic Marketing™ Resources

How to Cultivate, Nurture and Maintain Professional Relationships to Create Real Estate Clients for Life

To fully appreciate the power of voice broadcasting technology (see Chapter 6), put yourself in your prospect's shoes. Imagine you arrive home after a hard day's work and on your answering machine is the voice of a Presidential candidate with a succinct message about an issue important to you with a request for your vote. Got your attention?

Okay, so maybe you're not running for President, but imagine that you and your spouse are considering purchasing a new home and before you even consider contacting an agent, you receive a friendly message from a local Realtor informing you of current mortgage interest rates and new listings.

You press "erase" on your answering machine and decide to postpone a decision until later. But before you can reconsider, another message from the same Realtor appears on your answering machine. The following month, another message arrives. You say, "WOW! This agent really wants my business." And when your prospect says "WOW"…you win!

In an ideal world, you could easily execute this kind of marketing strategy by simply cloning yourself and adding an additional 18 hours to your work day. However, in the real world, there simply isn't enough time or resources to contact each prospect and past client individually. But what a tremendous benefit (not to mention lucrative opportunity) if you could!

Well, now you can! As I discussed earlier in Chapter 6, by using Voice Broadcasting on a regular basis, you can expand your personal relationships with your clients…*creating clients for life.* Looking for new clients? Voice broadcasting is a powerful tool for prospecting (my company, The Hartman Media Company, will formulate a program for you if you don't have one)

Implement The Two Keys
Of Every Successful Business Owner

Create Systems to Run Your Business—
You Run the Systems

In my business, competition is fierce. Fewer and fewer agents are doing more and more of the business. In fact, 80% of all transactions are done by less than 20% of the Realtor community. Part of the reason for this is that *top producers* are constantly looking for new and innovative systems to increase the productivity of their businesses. They can scale their efforts by running the systems which run their businesses, enabling them to work *smarter* rather than harder.

They make a clear distinction between *activity* and *productivity.* The systems allow them to focus on the productivity-oriented aspects of their businesses and leave the routine activity-oriented chores to their automated systems.

For example, imagine that every month you downloaded new leads gathered via the World Wide Web into your voice broadcast system. Then you send out your prospective homebuyer message to these leads in mere seconds…each prospect receives a call. No lead falls through the cracks and becomes lost. Then you queue up your farm database message – a friendly monthly update to your past clients. The message is sent in just seconds…and each past client receives a call to nurture your existing relationships.

Exceed Expectations by Creating Unique Selling Propositions

To separate themselves from the faceless crowd, *top producers* apply innovative techniques and strategies that practically compel prospects to do business with them.

Imagine you're at your next listing appointment and you are demonstrating your 24-hour lead generation system. You show your prospects how your system generates 4 to 5 times the buyer inquiries than traditional advertising would generate. You demonstrate how effectively and efficiently you follow up and how precisely you track the responses to their property, helping to ensure the sale. Then you show your listing prospect your Voice Broadcast system and demonstrate how ingeniously and repetitively their listing will generate exposure to every active buyer in the market.

Then your competition shows up and tells the prospect that they will put the home in the Multiple Listing Service and put a sign on the front lawn.

Who is exceeding the prospect's expectations and is creating a unique selling proposition? Who do you think will get the listing?

Using Voice Broadcast With Direct Mail

Fewer than one in five direct mail pieces are read. If you mail postcards, the exposure you receive before the recipient throws your postcard into the trash is less than five seconds.

Imagine sending a direct mail piece offering a free report to be sent in a non-threatening way via Voice Broadcast technology. First you call each prospect individually saying, "look for this very important report." Would this exceed their expectations and create a unique offer? Sure, but you don't have the time to call everyone individually and send out every report.

With voice broadcasting, you can implement this marketing strategy with a ten minute investment, and at a cost of pennies per contact! Your system will deliver the report and even capture the necessary prospect information for effective follow up. As an added bonus, the automated message will give you perhaps 25 seconds exposure – over five times the exposure the average post card receives.

Voice Broadcast Versus Telemarketing

Everyone knows that telemarketing works, but nobody relishes the thought of doing it. Some blame laziness, some blame the inability to handle repeated rejection.

The prevailing perception of telemarketers among the general population is that is that they are unprofessional and intrusive. Is it any wonder that telemarketers are often met with stiff resistance? It's tough to find a good telemarketer...and even tougher to keep one. However, the telephone is widely recognized as one of the most powerful tools at the sales professional's disposal. Suppose you could harness telemarketing's effectiveness while eliminating its resistance and minimizing its cost.

Voice broadcasting penetrates a higher percentage of your prospect database than a telemarketer could and your entire sales message is heard. Since the message is recorded, there is no variance – it is perfect every time! You don't have to worry about your telemarketer having a bad day and presenting you in an unprofessional manner. You maintain proper voice inflection, enthusiasm and tonality on every call. Your message is consistent and powerful.

VOICE BROADCAST WITH POWERLINE!

Using the techniques and strategies of Powerline, you will generate 300-500% more opportunities than with traditional advertising.

Have you ever thrown out leads because you simply couldn't follow up? Have leads ever gone cold because you or your staff just couldn't get to them in time? With so many leads, it's tough to find the time to stay in touch with so many clients and prospects. Voice broadcasting makes it possible.

By downloading the leads from your Powerline via the Internet and loading them directly into your Voice Broadcast System, you'll ensure timely follow up. You'll eliminate lost revenue and cold leads. You'll be able to send a message to every lead within minutes. You'll be able to make initial contact while the prospect's interest is at its peak.

Together, Powerline and Voice Broadcast make a natural, compelling combination!

VOICE BROADCAST FEATURES

Voice Broadcast Technology

One of the most state-of-the-art evolving technologies on the market! A proprietary network composed of completely non-blocking communication lines. Every call is connected through ISDN signal lines, digitally processed and capable of handling thousands of calls per hour every day!

Voice Broadcast Scripts

Your system comes complete with lead generation scripts specific to discovering new listings, uncovering potential homebuyers, expireds and FSBO's. Client messaging scripts nurture and maintain your existing business, ensuring clients for life!

Recorded Messaging

The system differentiates between an answering machine or voice mail and a live answer. When the system reaches an automated machine it leaves the message you recorded. When the call is answered by a person you have the option of having the system leave an alternative recorded message such as "sorry, wrong number" or simply hanging up. The recipient cannot trace terminated calls.

Electronic Loading of Database Via Email

A secure server automatically loads your database files within minutes of receipt. You control the list loading, managing and naming of lists. The system sends a confirmation message via email when your list is loaded and ready for broadcasting.

Customized Prospect Databases Available

Your list can be customized for approximately $99. You can extrapolate as many prospecting lists from this one master list as you desire, virtually guaranteeing a lifetime of leads!

Configurable Start-Stop Times for Broadcasting

You can configure the start day and time and ending day and time for each list to avoid sending broadcasts during hours when live answers are likely. You can configure and queue as many databases as you desire.

Real Time Call Detail Reporting via Fax or the World Wide Web

Call report is immediately available detailing successful messages delivered or failed (due to live answer, no machine, busy or bad number) with documentation for follow up and updating of your databases.

RATE PLAN
$295 Activation Fee
- Completed calls - 15 cents per minute billed in six second increments
- 12-second minimum per answered call
- $10 monthly service fee as an add-on to Powerline or Home Affordability Line
- $20 monthly service fee as stand-alone service

If you are not in touch with your clients then you are out of touch with your clients. If you are out of touch with your clients then they are out of touch with you. If they are out of touch with you then you are not the first person they think of when they have a need for real estate services or have friends or relatives in need of real estate services.

For more information about Voice Broadcast or other great marketing programs and services, visit www.BrandofChoice.com.

Prices and terms are subject to change without prior notice

Voice Broadcast Service Agreement

Product Description: Arch Telecom Voice Broadcast provides the ability for a Customer to record personalized voice messages and deliver the messages to a list of telephone destinations provided by the Customer. All destinations and recordings provided will remain private and will not be used or distributed in any manner by Arch Telecom, except as required by law. The Service Agreement and the Terms and Conditions set forth therein are between Arch Telecom Voice Broadcast Service and the subscribing Customer, and The Hartman Media Company has no liability or responsibility thereunder.

Representation of Telemarketing Compliance: The Federal Telephone Consumer Protection Act of 1992, and all revisions thereto ("TCPA") regulate the use of telecommunications for marketing products and services. The Customer represents and warrants that any and all actions taken by the Customer pursuant to this Service Agreement shall be in compliance with the TCPA.

Please fax completed form to:

**The Hartman Media Company
Fax: (949) 552-7001**

Customer Information:

Name _____

Company _____

Address _____

City _____ State ____ Zip _____

Phone (_____) _____

Fax (_____) _____

Email _____

Party Responsible for Charges _____

Setup Fee:

To activate service and receive the product materials, the following one-time setup fee applies.

Standard Voice Broadcast Setup Fee $295.00*

* prices subject to change without notice

Payment for Setup Fee

(attach Check OR complete the credit card payment information)

Card No _____ Expires _____

Card Name _____

Signature _____

Usage Charges:

Usage charges for the Service will be billed monthly. Sales and Usage taxes will be assessed where applicable. All long-distance charges will be assessed the 4.25% FCC Universal Service Fund tax.

- Monthly Service Fee for this service is $20.00. If the Customer has an existing account with Arch, the current service fee will be increased by this amount. Service fee for new accounts is waived for thirty (30) days following order date.
- Per Minute Usage rate is $0.150 billed in six-second increments (twelve-second minimum) for domestic calls. International rates are available upon request. Billable calls will include all calls answered, whether by machine or live person and calls administering the system. Zero-transfer, Survey or other enhanced services may be more. Only unanswered / busy calls are non-billable. Cost estimates for jobs are available via the Arch web site.

Monthly Usage Payment Method – Check One

❏ Automatic Credit Card debit – Account charges for each month will be automatically charged on the first business day of each month to the credit card provided below. If unbilled charges exceed $500, Arch may charge such amounts prior to the end of the month. The customer will receive a detailed invoice for record keeping.

Card No _____ Expires _____

Card Name _____

Signature _____

❏ Deposit with Invoice for payment Net 30 – Minimum deposit of $500 or 50% of outstanding charges, whichever is greater. Account will be billed monthly for charges. Payments are due within 30 days to avoid late fees and suspension of services. Deposit must be submitted with order to activate service and will be refunded within 15 days of closing account.

Optional Configuration

Special: _____

_____

_____

_____

Customer Authorization

I certify that I have read and understand and agree to be bound by this Service Agreement and the Terms and Conditions of Arch Telecom. I also certify that I am authorized to act on behalf of the Responsible Party indicated above.

Signed: _____ Date: _____

For Office Use

ARP / Rep_____JHS/JHS_____ Source _____(none)_____

Order#_____ Account _____

DNIS _____

Assignments _____

Please fax completed form to:
   The Hartman Media Company
   Fax: (949) 552-7001

Terms and Conditions:

Service

1. Any services assigned to you (including toll-free numbers, mailbox numbers, listing numbers) will remain the property of Arch. Any services transferred to Arch by you upon ordering service will be released by Arch upon full settlement of outstanding charges.
2. Arch makes no guarantees as to the continuous availability of the Service or any specific feature of the Service. Arch reserves the right to change the Service or any of its features at any time with or without notice.

Fees, Charges and Money Back Guarantee

3. By accepting this Agreement, you agree that you are responsible for all charges posted to your account until you cancel the account as specified in Section 24. The usage charges will include calls made in the administration of your services. In addition, the use of toll-free numbers may result in unintended calls (wrong numbers, etc) and charges to your service for which you are responsible.
4. The money back guarantee, where offered, provides solely that the Setup Fee will be refunded within 90 days of ordering the Service if not satisfied. The condition of this guarantee is that you actively used the Service to allow a reasonable evaluation of the Service benefits. If you have not actively used the Service, Arch will refund the Setup Fee less $100 for order processing costs. Refunds will be issued by check within 45 days of canceling the Service.
5. The rates and prices provided in the Service Agreement are not expected to change. However, Arch may change rates or institute new fees at any time upon 30 days prior notice.
6. A service fee of $15.00 will be assessed to your account for each check that is returned to Arch for insufficient funds.
7. Payments for all charges are due within 30 days of the month in which charges are incurred. If your account is delinquent, your account may be suspended or cancelled at Arch's sole discretion. If your account is suspended, regular charges continue to accrue until you cancel your account. A late fee of $10.00 will be assessed to your account if payments are not received by the due date.
8. You agree to pay all sales and use taxes, duties, or levies which are required by law as well as all attorney and collection fees arising from efforts to collect any unpaid balance on your account.
9. If you believe Arch has billed you in error, you must contact Customer Service within 60 days of the invoice or transaction date of the charge. Refunds or adjustments will not be given for any charges which are more than 60 days old.

Use of the Service

10. You and your representatives are the only individuals who are authorized to administrate the Service. You must not permit anyone else to administrate your Service and must ensure that all authorized

users comply with this Agreement. You are responsible for maintaining the confidentiality of passwords used for your account.

11. You are responsible for all charges assessed as a result of the use of your account. However, Arch will not hold you responsible for charges attributable to an unauthorized user's access to your account provided that you notify Arch within 24 hours of discovering any such unauthorized use and the unauthorized use is not attributable to the failure of any authorized user to exercise reasonable control over the confidentiality of the account or password.

12. You will not use or permit others to use the Service through your account in any way that violates any law or regulation; subjects Arch to liability; or is in contravention with these Terms and Conditions.

13. Monitoring the Service. Arch has no obligation to monitor the Service but may do so and may disclose information regarding your use of the service to satisfy laws, regulations or governmental requests. Arch, at it's sole discretion, may suspend service or refuse to provide service where Arch finds the use to be in violation of this Agreement.

14. You assume full responsibility and risk for use of the Service. The service is provided on an "AS IS" and "AS AVAILABLE" basis. Arch does not warrant that the Service will be uninterrupted or error-free. Arch makes no express or implied warranties, representations or endorsements including, but not limited to, warranties of title, non-infringement or implied warranties of merchantability or fitness for a particular purpose. No advice or information given by Arch, it's employees or affiliates shall create a warranty.

Your Remedies

15. If you are dissatisfied with the Service or any of its terms, conditions, rules, policies, guidelines or practices, your sole and exclusive remedy is to terminate this Agreement and discontinue using the Service by canceling your account.

16. Under no circumstances shall Arch, it's employees or affiliates be liable for any direct, indirect, incidental, special, punitive, or consequential damages that result in any way from any use of you account or the Service or your inability to use the Service.

17. Representation of Telemarketing Compliance – The Federal Telephone Consumer Protection Act of 1992, and all revisions thereto ("TCPA") regulate the use of telecommunications for marketing products and services. The customer represents and warrants to Arch that any and all actions taken by the Customer pursuant to this Service Agreement shall be in compliance with Houston, Texas with respect to all disputes arising out of this Agreement, your use of the Service or otherwise between you and Arch. Any cause of action you may have with respect to the Service must be commenced within one (1) year after the claim or cause of action arises or such claim or cause or action is barred.

18. Indemnity. Customer agrees to protect, defend, hold harmless and indemnify Arch from and against any losses, claims, demands, or causes of action or judgements related to or arising out of this Service Agreement, that are brought or may be brought against Arch arising out of this Service Agreement, including but not limited to violations of

the TCPA and any other federal or state telecommunications and/or telemarketing laws, even if such losses, claims, demands or causes of action or judgements are based on the sole, joint, or concurrent negligence or fault of Arch.

Term and Termination

19. Term of the Agreement. This Agreement is effective from your acceptance thereof, which is indicated by your first use of the Service through your account. If you are a current Arch member when this Agreement is activated, your continued use of the Service constitutes your acceptance of this Agreement.
20. You may terminate this Agreement by using only the methods outlined in the NOTICE section. Your termination will be complete upon receipt of a confirmation number from Arch. Your will receive verbal confirmation if you cancel by telephone, or a written reply if you cancel by fax or mail. Email cancellations will not be accepted. Charges will stop accruing the day you receive your confirmation number. Arch does not issue pro-rata refunds for monthly service fees and charges.
21. Arch may terminate this Agreement at any time without cause upon 30 days prior notice; or, immediately upon notice if you, or any person who has access to the Service through your account, commit a material breach of this Agreement, including but not limited to failure to pay any charges with 30 days of the due date.
22. Termination of this Agreement does not release you from the obligation to pay all accrued charges under this Agreement.
23. Arch's right to enforce the provisions of this Agreement shall survive the termination of this Agreement.

Notices

24. You may change or cancel your Arch account by the following methods only: first-class registered or certified mail, return receipt requested address to Arch Telecom, 210 Barton Springs Rd., Suite 275, Austin TX 78704; or telephone calls directed to Customer Service at 800-882-9155. Arch has no obligation, but may respond to notices delivered by facsimile or email to Arch.
25. Arch may provide you notice with the following methods: Electronic mail addressed to your email account; general posting to Arch's website at http://www.archtelecom.com; or by US Mail or courier service at the address you provided Arch when you ordered the Service. All notices shall be deemed effective on the first (1st) calendar day following the date of electronic posting or on the fourth (4th) calendar day following the date of sending by mail or courier.

Miscellaneous

26. Arch's failure to enforce strict performance of any provision of this Agreement shall not be construed as a waiver.
27. This Agreement shall be governed by and construed in accordance with the laws of the State of Texas, United States of America, without regard to its conflicts of law provisions. You consent to the personal jurisdiction of the federal and state courts having jurisdiction for Houston, Texas

with respect to all disputes arising out of this Agreement, your use of the Service or otherwise between you and Arch. Any cause of action you may have with respect to the Service must be commenced within one (1) year after the claim or cause of action arises or such claim or cause or action is barred.

28. Any action at law, suit in equity, or other judicial proceeding concerning, relating to, or arising from, or touching upon in any way, no matter how remotely, the contract for services between you and Arch Telecom, Inc. and/or your use of and/or Arch's provision of systems and services thereunder, shall be brought and litigated, if at all, only in the state court system of the State of Texas. In such event, you acknowledge the right of the specified court to asset personal jurisdiction in any such action over you and waive and release now and forever any defense to that assertion of jurisdiction that might otherwise exist.

29. Neither this Agreement, nor any of your rights or obligations arising hereunder, shall be transferred by you to any third party without Arch's prior written consent.

30. This Agreement and the Terms and Conditions constitute the entire agreement between you and Arch with respect to the Service.

31. Arch reserves the right to alter, amend or modify this Agreement at any time upon thirty (30) days notice. No amendment or modification to this Agreement by you shall be binding on Arch unless made in writing and signed by both parties.

Resources & Bibliography

Alessandra, Dr. Tony; "How To Increase Your Charisma Quotient," Nightingale-Conant.

Anderson, Stephen; "Automated Marketing: The Key to Profits in Your Future," Smart Marketing, Inc.

Anderson, Stephen; "Ten Biggest Marketing Mistakes Almost Every Business Makes," Smart Marketing, Inc.

Blake, George; "The Perfect Name," Probus Publishing.

Blum, Arnold; "How a Personal Computer Can Increase Your Sales," Smart Marketing, Inc.

Buffini, Brian, Templeton, Tim, "Working by Referral."

Chevron, Jacques; "Give Your Brand in Marriage," Advertising Age, July 1985.

Chevron, Jacques; "Branding and Promotion: An Uneasy Cohabitation," Brand Week, Sept. 14, 1998.

Chevron, Jacques; "The Delphi Process: Strategic Branding Methodology," Journal of Consumer Marketing, summer 1998.

Christian, Nichole; "Chrysler's 'Jeep Jamboree' Lives Hype of Jeep Commercials," The Wall Street Journal.

Cialdini, Robert, "Principles of Ethical Influence." New Information Presentations.

Cope, Dan; "Bonus Clubs Boom as Marketers Seek to Keep Customers," Kiplinger Magazine, April 13, 1994.

Daemon, Jane; "A Bird in the Hand; Marketing Success in the 21st Century," Industry Week, March 2, 1998.

Dossey, M.D., "The Power of Prayer."

Fisher, Jerry; "The Secret's Out: Relationship Marketing," Entrepreneur, May '98.

Garrity, Tom; "Garrity Brandbuilders: A Technique to Set You Apart," Garrity Communications, Inc.

Gordon, Ian; "Relationship Marketing-Your Vital Role," The Selling Advantage, summer, 1998.

Gordon, Ian; "Relationship Marketing"; John Wiley & Sons.

Gruen, Thomas; "Relationship Marketing - the Emperor in Used Clothing," Business Horizons, Nov. 1997.

Meyerson, Richard; "The Boy in the Box."

Holland, Henry; "Relationship Marketing, -What's at Stake," Oats Marketing.

Horowitz, Bruce; "GM's Saturn Pushes Relationship Marketing with 2-day Fete," Times Mirror Company.

Kaufmann, Mel, "The Millionaire's Handbook." Kaufmann Publishing.

Landers, Peggy; "Stores Gear Up to Make Customers Feel at Home," Knight-Ridder.

McKenna, Regis; "Relationship Marketing: Successful Strategies for the Age of the Customer," Addison Wesley.

McGinn, Daniel; "Oh, What a Feeling," Newsweek, July 28, 1997.

McSweeney, Jack & Mabey, Mike; "What's Hot Today in Relationship Marketing," Target Response Systems.

Norman, Jan; Orange County Register Morning Business; July 15, 1996.

Peppers, Don; "Enterprise One to One: Tools for Competing in the Interactive Age," Currency/Doubleday.

Pribram, Karl, M.D., "The Neuropsychology of Achievement."

Reynolds, Josh, Times Mirror Co., Los Angeles CA; "New Strategies for DPOs."

Sanow, Arnold & McComas, Daniel; *Marketing Boot Camp*, Smart Business.

Sharp, David, "L.L.Bean Offers Classes for On-Going Customer Relationships," Times Mirror Company.

Skirving Brian; "100 Relationship Marketing Letters," Loyalty Magic, Inc.

Skirving, Brian; "Developing Your Own Loyalty Program," Loyalty Magic, Inc.

Vavra, Terry, "Aftermarketing: How to Keep Customers for Life,( )" Irwin Professional Publishing.

Weber, Stu; "Tender Warrior," Putnam & Sons.

Weisbrod, Carl S., Ph.D., "The Charismatic Realtor," The Weisbrod Digest of Seminars.

Index

List of Illustrations

Please visit our website

WWW.BRANDOFCHOICE.COM

for a **FREE** newsletter
and additional information on:

- Jason Hartman's Personal Coaching Program

- Booking Jason Hartman for Public Speaking engagements

- Ordering additional copies of this book and other Hartman Media Company Publications

ORDER FORM

4 Ways to Order:

(800) 431-1579 Toll Free

(949) 552-7001 Fax

www.BrandOfChoice.com

Jason Hartman
PMB 117
4482 Barranca Parkway, Suite 180
Irvine, CA 92604

Order by credit card, personal check:

_____ Copies at $19.95 each $ _____
($19.95 U.S. currency; $30.95 Canada)

Plus shipping/handling $ _____
$4.50 for first book
(U.S. currency; inquire for international shipping rates)

$2.00 for each additional book $ _____

Total enclosed $ _____

Send Books To:

Name _____

Address _____

City _____ State _____ Zip _____

_____ Visa   _____ MasterCard

Credit card number _____

Expiration date _____

Signature _____